handcraft
wire Jewelry
CHAINS · CLASPS · PENDANTS

Kimberly Sciaraffa Berlin

KALMBACH BOOKS

WAUKESHA, WI

Kalmbach Books
21027 Crossroads Circle
Waukesha, Wisconsin 53186
www.JewelryAndBeadingStore.com

Lettered step-by-step and design option photos by Curtis Potter. All other photography
© 2015 Kalmbach Books.

Published in 2015
19 18 17 16 15   1 2 3 4 5

Manufactured in China

ISBN: 978-1-62700-133-5
EISBN: 978-1-62700-134-2

Editor: Karin Van Voorhees
Book Design: Lisa Bergman
Illustrator: Kellie Jaeger
Photographer: William Zuback

Library of Congress Control Number: 2014958391

contents

Projects

introduction

Handcraft Wire Jewelry: Chains, Clasps, Pendants is an easy-to-follow introduction to wireworking techniques and embellishments designed to give you room to grow, create unlimited designs, and make your own stunningly unique jewelry. This book is organized to help you learn about wireworking tools, develop and extend your skills, and have fun forming ideas and creating your own miniature works of art. I hope you will be challenged to learn and apply more jewelry design techniques and embellishments to your work, and to continue to build your wireworking skills.

To begin, you'll learn about wire property, tools, techniques and the embellishments you will use to create the projects in this book and your own designs. These ideas have been tested and demonstrated in the wirework classes I teach, and the information is an excellent reference to access when you are working through your own design ideas. The techniques and embellishments are interchangeable and can be used with almost any project. Next, you'll find 10 of my favorite chain styles, 12 new pendant ideas, and 10 custom clasp patterns. Not only is chain versatile, it adds dimension to your work and provides a wonderful way to wear and display your pendants. Since the chains I have included in this book are sets of flexible links, it is very easy to mix and match them to create your own combinations. Advanced wireweaving techniques, including eight weave patterns, are found at the end of the projects. I always tell you what weave I've used, but feel free to mix and match these techniques based on the properties of your focal piece and your personal preference. Inspiration can sometimes be elusive, so I conclude the book with thoughts on the process I use to help me organize, design, and develop my own distinct jewelry. This is meant as a guide to help you to unleash your own jewelry inspiration and skills.

These projects are a jumping off place for your creativity and offer you the opportunity to personalize all of your pieces. Skill levels are mixed and the techniques in the book are designed to be interchangeable. Create the projects using the techniques shown for each, or by using what you have learned about blending techniques, embellishments, and materials to take your design in a whole new artistic direction. Use the gallery of more ideas following each project for inspiration to adapt and modify any of the projects to suit your own color combinations and preferences. Whether you are a beginner or an experienced wire artist, I hope you will find this book helpful in extending and enhancing your jewelry making aspirations and that you will use the ideas and techniques to develop ideas for your own stunning jewelry designs.

Kimberly Berlin

materials

Wire

Shapes
Wire is fabricated in many shapes (round, half-round, square, triangular, twisted, and rectangular). The projects in this book use various gauges of round and half-round wire.

Types
You can purchase many types of wire to for jewelry making. Wire is available in gold, gold-filled, sterling silver, German silver, copper, brass, and various base metal mixtures. Sterling silver (92.5% silver and 7.5% base metal) or copper (99.9% copper) may be used for any of the projects in this book. Copper is the softest and least expensive of the available wires. It is cost effective and I find it to be very beautiful, especially when patina is added to a woven piece showcasing the weave work. Copper workability properties are very similar to silver. Permanently colored copper wire can also be used in some of the projects. It is pliable, comes in many colors, and can be used for many accent and weaving techniques. I do not recommend hammering the permanently colored, filled, coated, or plated wire because the nature of hammering causes the wire to flatten and spread exposing the metal inside.

Tempers
Temper refers to the malleability of the wire. There are three types of wire temper produced: dead soft, half-hard, and hard. The more you work with wire the more it hardens or stiffens and can eventually become brittle. This is called *work hardening*. Dead soft wire is used for all the projects in this book.

Gauges
Wire comes in many different gauges. The gauge of the wire is the size or diameter of the wire. The higher the number gauge the finer or thinner the wire. The American Standard Wire Gauge runs from the smallest gauge of 38 to the largest gauge of 1. The projects in this book generally call for wire gauges between 16 and 28. Sixteen- and 18-gauge wire can be used to create strong chain. For finer work, such as weaving and sewing beads and stones, much thinner wire (24, 26, or 28 gauge) is used.

Beads and Cabochons
One of the first things you must realize when choosing a cabochon or bead is that not all of them are created equally. I like to purchase and always have on hand a big stash of all kinds of cabochons and beads from which to choose. Beads come in a wide variety of shapes and kinds. For the purposes of this book, I focus on standard drilled, top-drilled, and front-drilled beads. Cabochons also come in a plethora of types, sizes, and shapes. But unlike beads, they do not have a drilled hole anywhere.

▲ Top Drilled
Top-drilled beads have a hole drilled through the top portion of the bead going from side to side.

▲ Standard Drilled
These beads have a hole drilled lengthwise, from the top to the bottom of the bead.

▲ Front Drilled

Front-drilled beads have a center hole drilled at the top of the bead going from the back through to the front.

▲ Cabochons

A cabochon, or *cab*, is a stone or larger focal piece that does not have a hole drilled through it. Cabs are generally flatter on the back, domed on the front, and have a small edge all the way around the sides. Cabochons need some sort of encasement to stay attached to metal or wire, such as a wire bezel, prongs, or a wire cage.

Tools

These tools can be found at your local bead store. Good tools will last you a very long time and will help you to produce better results. Purchase the highest quality tools you can afford that feel comfortable in your hands.

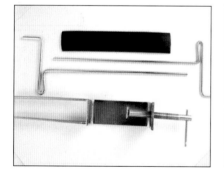 

▼ Tape

Blue, easy-release, non-residue painters tape is a staple for bezel wrapping cabochons and holding base wires in place while weaving or adding components. Use ¾-in. painter's tape for the projects in this book.

▲ Coiling Tools and Mandrels

Mandrels are used to wrap wire around to shape it, create jump rings, or to coil. Commonly, mandrels are made from metal rods, but they can also be made from many common household items such as dowels, prescription medication bottles, and pens. Most coiling tools contain mandrels of varying sizes. I prefer to use a coiling tool to make longer coils or double-coiled beads because it takes me far less time and the coils are uniform.

▶ Nylon or Rubber Head Hammer or Mallet

Use this to work harden wire. Because of the soft head, it will not scratch or mar metals.

▶ Picks and T Pins

Picks, wooden cuticle sticks, and T pins come in very handy. I use them to separate a weave that I have inadvertently overlapped or to open up an area where I need space for another piece of weave wire. I do this by carefully inserting the tip where I want space and moving it back and forth until it goes under or moves apart the overlapped wires. Sometimes my weave wires need to be a little closer together and I can also slide them over with a pick.

◀ Patina Removers

Patina results from a chemical reaction and adds color and depth to almost any jewelry piece. Sometimes you may need to bring out highlights in the jewelry by removing some of the color. I use different kinds of removal materials depending on my piece of jewelry and the finish effect I wish to achieve. Some of my staples are scouring pads, standard sanding blocks, soft brass brushes, and pro-polish pads. My preferred choice is the pro-polish pad because it is flexible, small, and doesn't leave any fibers stuck in my jewelry.

▲ Tumbler

A rotary or vibratory tumbler can be used to remove light scratches, clean, and add luster to most metals. Use the tumbler about one third full of mixed media stainless steel shot, add one drop of baby shampoo, and add water to cover the shot and pieces you are tumbling. Tumbling time varies according to the materials to be tumbled. Jewelry pieces containing delicate, soft, or porous stones are not suitable for tumbling.

▲ Bench Block

A bench block is a very smooth square piece of hardened, stainless steel and is used as a surface for hammering metals. Bench blocks come in different sizes. A 4x4-in. bench block is adequate for making most jewelry projects. To hammer using a bench block, place the wire on the bench block and use the flat end of the chasing hammer to flatten the wire.

▲ Flush Cutters

Flush cutters are used to cut wire almost flat ended. This makes it easier for you to file and helps to eliminate burs. Wire cutters have two sides; one flat and one concave. Cutting with the flat side of the cutter against your work creates a flush cut or almost flat cut. When cutting wire, normally the concave side of the cutter faces against the waste end. A very good flush cutter will save you lots of extra filing time in the long run.

▲ Flatnose Pliers

Flatnose pliers are used to create sharp bends in wire, holding wire, and opening and closing jump rings. These pliers have flat tapered faces on both sides of the jaws.

▲ Chainnose Pliers

Chainnose pliers have tapered jaws that are flat on the inner surface and curved on the outer surface. They come in many lengths and widths. Use this plier for sewing wire, pulling, and getting to hard-to-reach places within your work.

▲ Permanent Marker

A permanent marker, such as a fine-tipped Sharpie, can be used to mark measurements on the wire and on your tools. These markings can be polished off with a polishing cloth or are removed in a tumbler.

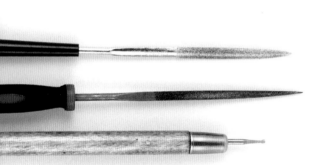

▲ Files and Wire Rounder

Small files or wire-rounders are used to smooth the ends of wire and clean up burs after the wire has been trimmed and is ready to use. Because most jewelry files have the coarse grain cut in one direction, you should file in one direction, against the grain of the file. Wire rounders (small cup burs). also come in many sizes and are used to smooth and shape the ends of wire.

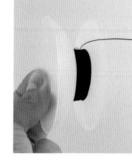

Bobbins

No-tangle thread bobbins such as those used for macramé and kumihimo can also be used to load fine wire for weaving purposes. The bobbin holds the wire in place, helps to eliminate kinking, and keeps wire from tangling or unraveling as you weave. I also find it much easier to weave with a bobbin when I need to apply a little tension on my weave wire.

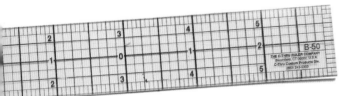

▲ Ruler

A ruler with both standard and metric markings, with a deep center tray is preferable. It is easier to roll out and measure wire along a larger tray.

▶ Polishing Cloth or Pad

Jewelry polishing cloths contain polishing compounds and can be used for cleaning and eliminating tarnish. Polishing jewelry with a polishing cloth helps it to resist tarnish to some degree because some of the polishing chemicals remain on the jewelry. Pro-polish pads have an abrasive and can also be used to remove tarnish.

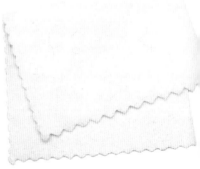

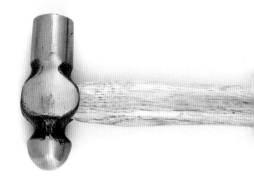

▲ Texture Hammer

A texture hammer is used to make decorative marks on wire when hammering the wire. There are many different types of texture hammers on the market. The balled end of a chasing hammer is often used for texturing metal.

▲ Long-Tined Roundnose Pliers

Roundnose pliers have long rounded tapered jaws and are used for making loops and curves. For wirework, roundnose pliers with 1½-in. long jaws will give you a good choice of loop placement sizes. Mark the roundnose pliers: Starting from the tips, measure ¼-in. and mark the place with the permanent marker. Mark every quarter inch until you reach the back of the pliers (¼, ½, ¾, 1, 1¼ in.). By using these markings when placing the wire, you can more easily make consistent loops and curves.

▲ Bail Making and Stepped Pliers

Bail-making (above) and stepped pliers come in many sizes and are used to make loops, small quantities of jump rings, and bails. The jaws/barrels are generally different diameters thus giving you different size mandrel choices.

▲ Ball Peen Hammer

A ball peen hammer has a flat end and a balled end. You can flatten and spread wire with the flat end and texture the wire with the balled end. Hammering the wire will also strengthen it. Hammering wire can be used to create texture or used to work-harden the metal. When hammering to create a smooth look on the wire, make sure that the hammer and the bench block you are using are free from scratches or nicks of any kind. Scratches or nicks can transfer as texture to your metal.

▲ Safety Goggles

Wear safety goggles to protect your eyes from flying debris and wire cuttings.

▲ Magnifiers/Optivisor

Wearing magnifying glasses or an optivisor allows you to see your work up close, reduces eye strain, and helps you to see small imperfections so that you can more easily fix them.

extra safety tips

- Wear eye protection when working with metals and wire.
- Work in a well-ventilated space.
- When cutting wire, hold the wire and cut facing down toward your work table to keep flying bits of wire to a minimum.
- Take periodic rest breaks to stretch.
- Use tools and chemicals according to the manufacturer's specifications.

▲ Chasing Hammer

The chasing hammer has a large circular, slightly convex end and a balled end. The circular, slightly convex end works well for flattening, tapering, and hardening wire. The balled end can be used for texturing wire.

basics

Making simple loops, wrapped loops, spirals, and opening and closing jump rings are some of the basic skills necessary to extend your application of the new techniques and embellishments contained in this book. These basic instructions should easily give you a grasp of these skills.

◀ Sewing

This technique allows you to embellish and add dimension to your projects. Flush cut 4–12 in. of 24- or 26-gauge round wire. At one end of the wire, make a 90-degree bend 1 in. from the tip. This bend will be the wire tail you hold as you wrap the other end of wire around the frame. Place the wire bend over the frame and make at least three tight wraps around the frame with the other end. String beads or stones onto this piece of wire. Wrap the wire to another place on the frame, making at least three wraps. If you have more wire to work with, continue to sew beads until your design is complete.

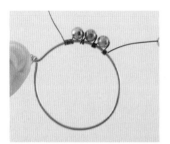

◀ Simple Edging

Edging a section or a whole piece is similar to sewing with the wire. To edge a piece or section, start with at least 8 in. of 24- or 26-gauge round wire. Make a small bend about ½ in. from one end of the wire. Hook the wire bend at the place where you wish to start the edging. Holding the short tail of the bend, use the longer end of the wire to wrap at least three times around where you wish to start the edging. String a small bead onto the long wire and let it drop down to the wraps. Make at least two wraps on the frame where you will continue to edge. Continue the process until you have completed edging.

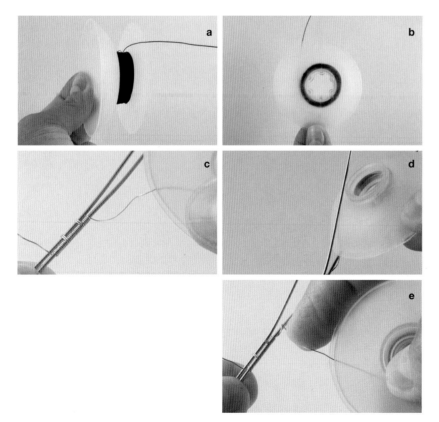

◀ Bobbin Weaving

Holding the bobbin, pull open the two ends until the bobbin ends stay open in place. Cut the length wire you wish to load onto the bobbin and wind it around the bobbin **a** until only about a 2-in. tail of wire is left. Close the bobbin sides together capturing the 2-in. tail so that it is left sticking out of the bobbin **b**. The wire should feed easily from the bobbin as you use it to weave **a**. Keep the length of wire feeding from the bobbin short as you weave **c**. Palming the bobbin, keep a steady tension as you push down your weave wire **(d, e)**.

▶ Simple Loop

Holding roundnose pliers on a flat plane, place the wire between the plier jaws at the ¼-in. mark **a**. You should be able to feel the tip of the wire barely sticking out of the top of the pliers. The longest portion of wire should be flowing out from the bottom of the pliers. Keeping the pliers flat and not moving, grasp the longest piece of the wire and pull it toward you and over the top of the pliers **b**. Stop when the wire is flat across the top of the pliers **c**. Remove the wire from the pliers. If your loop is not closed all the way, put the wire back in the plier and push it closed.

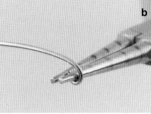

▶ Wrapped Loop

With flatnose pliers, make a 90-degree bend in the wire at least 2 in. from the end of the wire **a**. With roundnose pliers, grasp the end of the wire and roll the wire to make a complete loop **b**. Hold the loop flat in the jaws of flatnose pliers and use chainnose pliers to tightly wrap the tail of the wire around the neck of the wire. Make the wraps close together and tight. Trim any excess wire and using chainnose pliers, tuck in the wire tail against the base wire **c**.

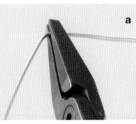

▶ Double Wrapped-Loop Link

For a double wrapped-loop, follow the directions for a wrapped loop. String a bead onto the wire and up against the first wrapped loop **a**. Make another wrapped loop at the other end of the wire and up against the bead **b**. Trim any excess and tuck in the tail **c**.

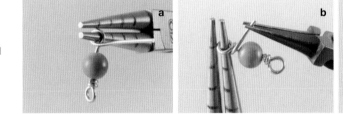

▶ Double Wrapped-Loop Caged Bead Link

Follow the directions for a double wrapped loop link. From the second wrapped loop, continue to wrap the wire tail back up and around the bead until the wire tail is back at the first set of wraps **(a, b)**. Wrap the wire tail around the first wrapped loop **c**. Trim any excess wire and tuck in the tail **d**.

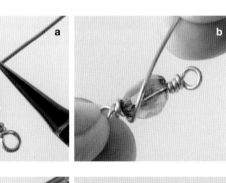

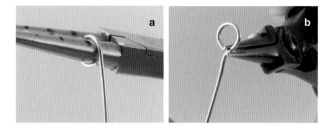

◀ Eye Loop

With roundnose pliers, make a simple loop **a.** Using chainnose pliers, grasp the inside wire across from the cut on the loop wire end and put a slight bend up and over to center the loop **b.** Open an eye loop just as you would a jump ring.

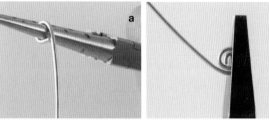

◀ Jump Rings

Place a pair of flatnose pliers on either side of the join (cut). in the jump ring. Open the jump ring by pushing the ends away from each other in opposite directions **(left)**. Do not pull open a jump ring, as it will lose shape. When closing the jump ring, use the same pushing motion. You should hear a faint click when the jump ring is snapped tightly closed. I sometimes use a larger gauge jump ring as a bail.

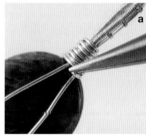

◀ Spirals

To start the spiral, make a simple loop at one end of the wire with roundnose pliers **a.** Using flatnose pliers, continue shaping the wire to start a second loop around the first. Using flatnose pliers, hold the spiral and turn it while guiding the wire around with your fingers, pushing the wire around and against the previous spiral **b.** Repeat the step by re-gripping the spiral and continue to shape the wire until the spiral is complete. Work in small movements to control the shape of the spiral curves. Leaving some space between the spiral rotations will create an open spiral.

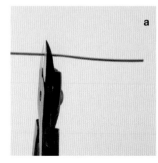

◀ Tucking

Tucking in a wire end is important when creating a professional and clean looking piece of jewelry. It also makes the jewelry piece more stable and less apt to snag and pull apart. Find a place or point on your jewelry piece to position a tucked wire end. Trim the wire end so that just enough is left to tuck in. Put a slight bend in the end of the wire to be tucked, and push the wire into the opening **a.** Squeeze it in place with chainnose pliers so the tuck appears seamless **b.**

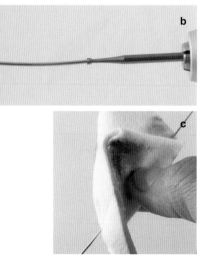

◀ Flush Cutting, Finishing Ends, and Straightening

Wire cutters have two sides: one flat and one concave. Cut with the flat side of the cutter against your work or toward the end you want to be flush to create a flush cut or almost flat cut. When cutting the wire, the concave side of the flush cutters should face against the waste end of the wire **a.** To further smooth the ends of the wire, use a wire file or a cup bur **b.** For the purposes of this book, all cuts should be flush and all ends should be filed smooth. Use a polishing cloth for easy cleaning and straightening **c.**

▶ Clasps

Clasps are the finishing touches at the ends of necklaces and bracelets that hold the ends together. They are not only functional, but can be artistic and decorative statement pieces. Most of the featured clasps have a hook-and-eye component. When the eye is not illustrated, use a jump ring in its place.

tips

- Hammering a finished clasp will make it stronger.
- Clasps are easily attached to the end of necklaces with jump rings. For a finished look, match the gauge jump ring to the wire gauge of the clasp.
- Match the shape of your hook to the shape of your chain links.
- Because clasps usually rest on the back of a neck or wrist, flush cut, tuck, and file away any rough places or burs that could be uncomfortable.

▶ Patina

Liver of sulfur can add an antique-looking finish to your pendants. It comes in three forms: dry chunks in a can, ready-to-use liquid, and gel. It does not take much of any of these types to add patina to a small project. I prefer to use patina gel. Liver of sulfur is non-toxic, but very stinky. Use it in a well-ventilated area and follow the manufacturer's directions. Each batch of liver of sulfur will produce different results and colorations. For the best results, use the same batch of liver of sulfur to patina all the parts of each project. For this book, adding patina is optional.

▶ Hammering and Texture

Place a bench block on a piece of smooth cloth or bench block pad, so that when you hammer, the force of the strike remains in the block and the noise is reduced.

tip
Use a piece of old polishing cloth as the buffer. Because it is soft, it will not damage the bench block, and doubled, it is thick enough to mute the sound. Use the convex, smooth side of a chasing hammer to flatten, harden, and create a smooth finish on the wire or use the balled end of the hammer to create texture. By focusing on where you are hammering, you can be very specific about which areas are textured or left smooth. A textured piece can be accented with patina. The patina will stay in the crevices of the textured parts.

beaded double
spiral chain

The beaded double spiral chain is easily one of my favorites. It is versatile, can easily be adapted, and can accommodate different bead shapes and colors for very different looks. I love to make matching earrings and a pendant to wear with this fabulous chain.

: materials

- 66-in. piece of 18-gauge round wire
- **22** 8mm donut shaped disk beads with holes large enough for 18-gauge wire
- **4** 23.6x2.7mm open oval jump rings
- **21** 3mm 18-gauge round open jump rings

: tools

- long-tined roundnose pliers
- 6mm bail-making pliers or mandrel
- flatnose pliers
- chainnose pliers
- flush cutters
- chasing hammer
- bench block
- small file or wire rounder
- permanent marker
- ruler
- polishing cloth

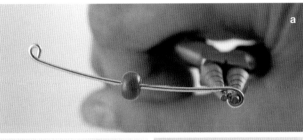

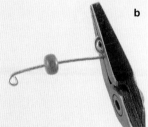

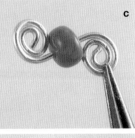

1 Flush cut a 2½-in. piece of 18-gauge round wire and mark the center of the wire.

2 Halfway between the tip and the ¼-in. plier mark, using roundnose pliers, make a simple loop at one end of the wire. String the bead onto the wire. Make a second simple loop to match the first at the opposite end of the wire **a**. These loops should be facing on opposite sides of the wire.

3 With flatnose pliers, spiral each side equally **b** until the wire is touching the bead on each side. Make sure the spirals are of equal revolutions and size **c**. Hammer each spiral. Make 20.

4 Attach an oval jump ring to each end of each spiral link though each link's spiral center. Use a round jump ring to connect the oval jump rings **d**.

5 Make a spiral, beaded clasp (p. 18).

6 Attach the clasp halves to each end of the necklace with round jump rings.

7 Add patina, if desired, following manufacturer's instructions.

◄ Matching the burro creek jasper bezeled woven pendant to the burro creek jasper beaded double spiral chain creates a classic look.

► Chalcedony round beads in two sizes give this chain a fresh style.

◄ I used large black crystals, turned the chain link sideways, and used a double connector clasp with spiral hook (p. 19) to make a very substantial and rich looking bracelet.

spiral beaded clasp

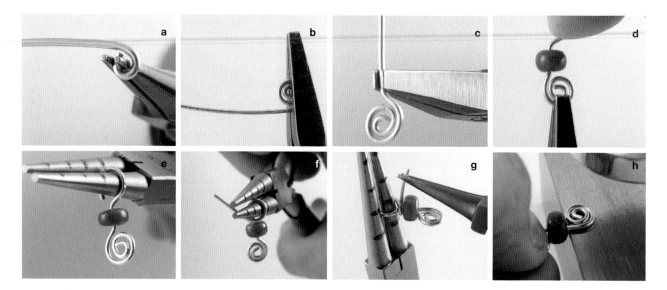

Hook

1 Flush cut a 2½-in. piece of 18-gauge round wire.

2 Using roundnose pliers, at the ¼-in. plier mark, make a simple loop at one end of the wire **a**.

3 Using flatnose pliers, spiral twice **b**.

4 With flatnose pliers, make a perpendicular bend in the wire at the top of the spiral **c**.

5 String a bead and make another bend so that the wire is pointing the same direction as the spiral **d**.

6 Using roundnose pliers, make a loop at the 1-in. plier mark **e**. Trim any excess wire even with the top of the bead to make a hook.

7 With a chasing hammer, gently hammer the spiral and hook. Because wire spreads as you hammer, reshape it if needed.

Eye

8 Flush cut a 3-in. piece of 18-gauge round wire. Repeat steps 2–5 of Hook.

9 Using roundnose pliers, make a wrapped loop at the ¾-in. plier mark **f, g**. Trim any excess wire even with the top of the bead.

10 Gently hammer the spiral and wrapped loop. Because wire spreads as you hammer, reshape it if needed.

11 Add patina if desired according to manufacturer's instructions.

double connector clasp with spiral hook

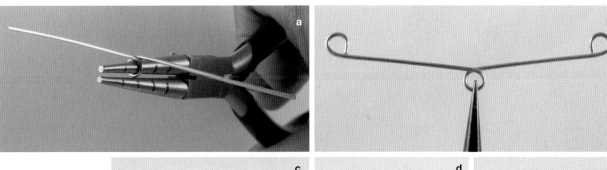

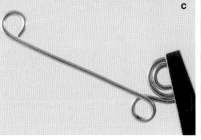

Hook and Connector

1 Cut a 4-in. piece of 18-gauge round wire and mark the center.

2 Using roundnose pliers at the ½-in. plier mark, make a loop on the center mark of the wire **a**.

3 Using roundnose pliers, at the ½-in. plier mark, make a simple loop at each end of the wire. These loops should face each other **b**.

4 With flatnose plies, spiral the loops in towards each other and to the center **c, d**.

5 Gently hammer the whole piece except where the wire crosses over itself. (Hammering the crossover weakens it.)

6 Make a spiraled S hook and attach it to the center loop with two jump rings **e**. (See spiraled S-hook clasp p. 35.)

Eye

7 Repeat steps 1–5 of the hook and connector instructions to make the eye.

orange dream basic bezeled woven pendant

I simply fell in love with this fossilized cabochon with its striking orange coloration and shapes that are reminiscent of a Monet painting. The bezel wrap on this cabochon was created with round wire. Normally, I use square wire to bezel wrap cabochons, but in this case, I added a woven component to the pendant. It is much easier to weave on round base wires than it is to weave on square base wires.

: materials

- 5 in. circumference/30x50mm oval cabochon
- 144 in. 28-gauge round wire
- 55-in. piece of 20-gauge round wire
- 20-in. piece of 20-gauge half-round wire
- 66-in. piece of 18-gauge round wire
- **28** 4mm round beads
- **27** 5.9mm oval open jump rings

: tools

- long-tined roundnose pliers
- 8mm bail-making pliers or mandrel
- flatnose pliers
- chainnose pliers
- flush cutters
- chasing hammer
- bench block
- small file or wire rounder
- small bobbin
- ruler
- permanent marker
- painters tape
- polishing cloth

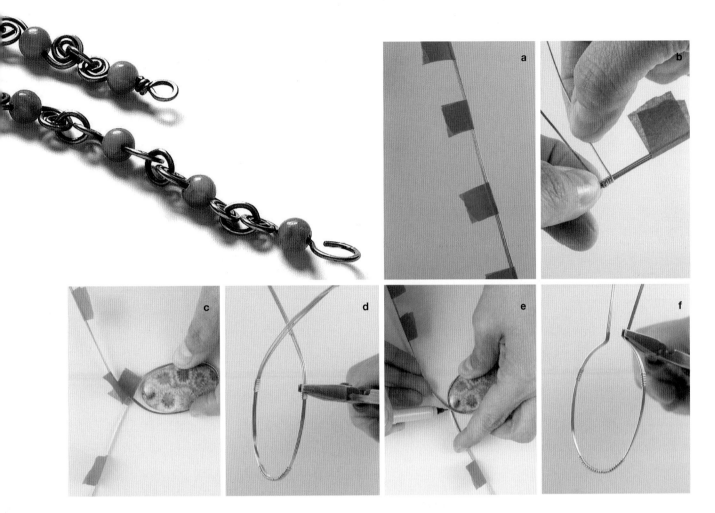

1 Flush cut three 17-in. pieces of 20-gauge wire. Line up the wires flat and flush, and place a piece of tape at one end to hold them in place. This is called a *bundle*. Wrap tape in three additional places on the same side of the wire bundle, with the tape flags facing in one direction **a**. This secures the bundle while you work on it. Measure and mark the center of the bundle.

2 Cut an 8-in. piece of 20-gauge half-round wire. With chainnose pliers, bend the wire in half with the flat side of the wire on the inside of the bend.

3 Hook the center bend of the half-round wire on the center of the marked bundle and hold it in place with your thumb. Begin wrapping the half-round wire snugly around the bundle. Make sure the wire wraps are close together and snug **b**. Be sure not to wrap too tight, as this will cause the base wires to overlap each other. After every two to three wraps, press the wire flat (crimp) with flatnose pliers. Be careful not to twist or bend the wire as you wrap it around the bundle. Make 13 wraps on each side of the center mark for a total of 26 wraps.

4 Use the flush cutters to trim the ends of the half-round wire. Make both binding-end cuts on the same side of the bundle. This becomes the inside of the bezel wrap; the cabochon pressing against these cuts will hold them in place.

5 Gently place and press the wire, with the cut-sides in, around the cabochon to determine the placement of two additional wrapped bindings **c**. Mark where you want to place the bindings on the wire. I placed the two binding marks on the wire about ¾–1-in. from the top of the cabochon.

note Bindings do not have to be symmetrical. Often, I purposefully accentuate a feature of a cabochon with asymmetrical binding placements.

6 Flush cut two 4-in. pieces of 20-gauge half-round wire and wrap the new binding markings as you did with the center binding wrap. There should be six total binding wraps on each side **d**. Trim any excess wire from the bindings. All of the binding-end cuts should be on the same side of the bundle (the inside facing the cabochon).

7 With the tape flags facing up, shape and press the wire bundle up and around the cabochon and mark where the wires cross **e**. Make sure the wrapped, binding-end cuts are all facing on the inside against the cabochon. Putting a gentle curve in the wire bundle before pressing it to the shape of the cabochon makes this process easier.

8 With flatnose pliers, bend the wires up at the marks **f**. Tape the wires together to hold them in place.

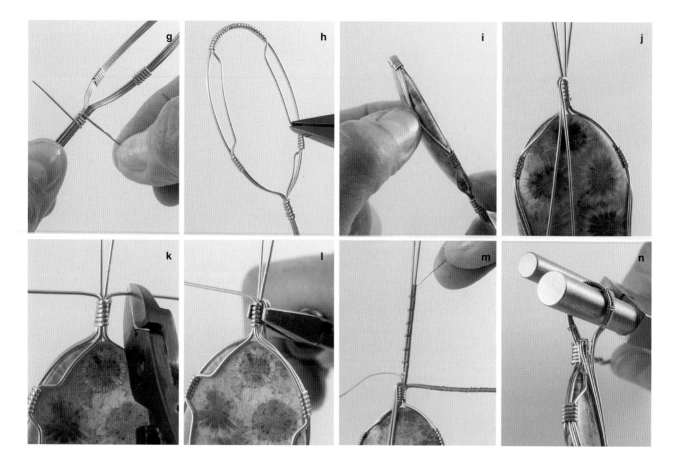

9 Flush cut one 4-in. piece of 20-gauge half-round wire. Wrap it at least six times or until it reaches the top of the bezel to bind both sides of the wire bundle **g**.

10 Remove all the tape flags but one. This piece of tape will tell you which side is the front of the wire bezel. The side of the bezel with the tape flag sticking out is the front of the frame and the side without a flag sticking out is the back of the frame. Create the back support wire bends for your cabochon. Hold the frame in your hand, place the tip of the flatnose pliers beside one wrapped binding on the back, grasp only one outside wire, and bend it to the inside **h**. Be careful not to change the shape of the wire bezel as you are holding it. Repeat this step until you have made at least three bends on the back of the frame. These bends will act like prongs to help hold your cabochon in the wire bezel.

11 Place the cabochon back in the frame. It should fit snugly. Make wire bends in the front of the cabochon to hold it in place. For this cabochon, I made gentle curved bends using two of the wires by gently pulling them forward with my fingernails and the flatnose pliers **i**.

12 Separate the top wires a little. Three wires in the bundle will yield six top wires. Bend the front two wires down to the front of the cabochon **j** and with the flatnose pliers, gently crimp them to the top wrap of the cabochon bundle.

13 Take the longest back wire and bend it at a sharp 90-degree angle from the top of the cabochon.

14 Separate the two middle wires from the rest of the wires. Mark these with tape so as not to confuse them from the rest of the top wires. These two wires will later become the bail. Bend the other back wire at a 90-degree angle out to the side and trim it to ⅛ in. **k**. Again, bend and crimp this cut wire to the side of the bail base and over the bail base wire wrap **l**.

15 Using the 28-gauge wire on a bobbin, coil (p. 89) on the remaining wire at the side, starting at the 90-degree bend and finishing about 1 in. from the end of the wire.

16 Start Weave 1 (p. 90) on the remaining two wires at the top of the cabochon wraps. Complete the Weave 1 pattern of coil ten on base wire 1, wrap two on base wires 1 and 2, do this for eight complete weave rotations **m**. Trim the weave tails.

17 With 8mm bail-making pliers placed about ¼-in. from the top of the cabochon, wrap the woven top wires over the bail-making pliers and onto the front of the cabochon **n**.

note Control the size of the bail by the mandrel size you choose.

18 Hold the bail top wires against the front of the cabochon. Using the wire that is coiled, bend a 90-degree angle out to the side. Wrap it tightly around the wires starting at the top and wrapping down.

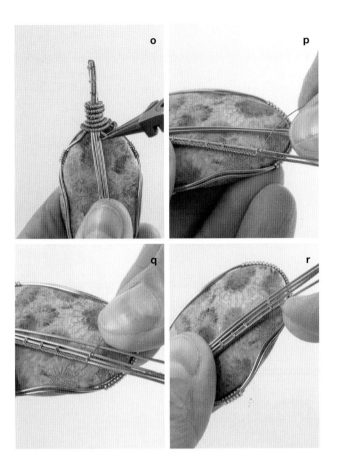

19 Stop wrapping when you reach the top of the cabochon and the bottom of the bail. Trim and tuck (p. 14) in the wire at the bottom of the wrapping **o**.

20 Using the 28-gauge bobbin wire, start Weave 1 at the top of the two wires closest to the side of the cabochon. Weave the pattern 10 coils on base wire 1, then two wraps on base wires 1 and 2, with seven complete weave rotations **p**. Trim and tuck any excess tails at the top of the weave.

21 Continue coiling 20 more coils on base wire 1 and start Weave 3 (p. 91), and capture all four wires **q**. Finish off Weave 3 with five coils on base wire 1 **r**. Trim and tuck the tails. Trim the three bottom wires to 1 in. each.

22 With flatnose pliers, gently lift the side prong wire, insert the first bottom wire underneath, and pull it through. With chainnose pliers, make a wrap onto the prong wire. Trim any excess wrap wire.

23 Spiral (p. 14) the remaining wires flat against the cabochon. Add patina, if desired, following manufacturer's instructions.

note
Make a matching chain to display your beautiful pendant. (See beaded double spiral chain p. 16.) Use the larger oval jump rings as connectors in place of the set of three jump rings used in the project.

more ideas

◀ For this petite Tabu Tabu Jasper cabochon, I made a small woven spiral on the front to accentuate the stone and show off the red spots.

▶ Texas Palm Wood is a beautiful stone and its color is enhanced by copper. For this variation, I wrapped the weave wires around to the back of the stone before sweeping them across and anchoring them to the front.

◀ For this beautiful druzy, I used longer wires so that I would have enough to encircle the cabochon with the wire before weaving my spiral.

▶ This is one of my favorites; a fun coprolite (Paleozoic dinosaur poo) cabochon. I made it more playful by adding coiled red beads to match the blood-red veining on the stone.

23

orbital figure-8 chain

The orbital figure-8 chain is beautiful in its simplicity and can be easily adapted in so many ways—in size, link combinations, or through mixed metals—to name a few. I love to use this chain with mixed metals and funky oversized links.

: materials

- 60-in. piece of 16-gauge round wire
- **88** 8mm outer diameter open jump rings

: tools

- long-tined roundnose pliers
- 7mm and 10mm mandrels or bail-making pliers
- flatnose pliers
- chainnose pliers
- flush cutters
- small file or wire rounder
- permanent marker
- ruler
- chasing hammer
- bench block
- polishing cloth

1 Flush cut a 2¼-in. piece of 16-gauge round wire. Using 6mm bail-making pliers, make a simple loop at one end of the wire **a**. Using 6mm bail-making pliers, place the simple loop on the mandrel and wrap the wire around the mandrel until the wire crosses over the center of the wire and past the first loop **b**. This makes a figure-8 shape. Trim the excess wire flush and touching the center of the wire **c**. Adjust with flatnose pliers so the ends are flush with the center **d**. Gently hammer the piece and because wire spreads as you hammer, reshape it if needed. Make 15.

2 Close one jump ring. Open a jump ring, pick up the closed ring, and close the open ring. Stack the linked rings. Use 88 jump rings to make 44 stacks **e**.

3 Using flatnose pliers, open one end of a figure-8 link and string jump ring stack. Center the jump rings in the middle portion of the figure 8 **f**, and close the link. Do this for all of this size figure-8 links.

4 With flatnose pliers, open one end of a figure-8 link and connect it through a jump ring stack. Close the link. Repeat with another figure 8, connecting the new figure 8 with the same jump ring stack **g**. Connect seven figure-8 links for one side of the chain and eight for the other side (the hook attaches to the shorter side).

note To illustrate how to connect the figure-8 links to each other, I used links without center stacks in photo g.

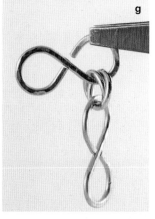

5 Flush cut a 3-in. piece of 16-gauge round wire. Using a 10mm mandrel, repeat step 1. Make seven of this size link.

Optional: Use the ball end of the chasing hammer to texturize the larger figure-8 links before connecting.

6 Using flatnose pliers, open one end of a figure-8 link and string a stack of jump rings. Center the jump rings in the middle of the figure 8. Repeat for all of this size figure-8 link.

7 Using flatnose pliers, open one end of a figure-8 link and connect it through a stack of jump rings. Repeat to connect another figure-8 link to the same stack. Connect all the figure-8 links this size to jump ring stacks. This becomes the center of the chain.

8 Using flatnose pliers, connect each smaller figure-8 link chain end to one side of the larger linked chain with a jump ring.

9 Flush cut a 2¼-in. piece of 16-gauge round wire. Using a 6mm mandrel or 6mm bail maker pliers, make a simple loop at one end of the wire. Using a 6mm mandrel or 6mm bail maker pliers, place the simple loop on the pliers and wrap the wire around the pliers until the wire touches the top of the simple loop. Trim the excess

wire at the end of the second loop so that the trim is even to the center of the first loop, put a small bend in the tip, and then hammer the whole hook **h**. Attach the hook to the end of the chain that has only seven of the smaller links. The eighth link becomes the eye on the other side of the chain.

10 Add patina, if desired, following manufacturer's instructions.

more ideas

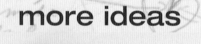

▲ I love to use mixed metals and this alternative is no exception. I made much smaller figure-8 links, attached them to very large figure-8 links, used figure-8 links as connector links, and accentuated the center of each link with sterling silver jump rings.

▼ These two earring pairs have similar compositions. Each have beaded edging, texturized figure-8 links, and sewn-in center-focal beads. These are fun to make, wear, or give as gifts. They are great holiday accessories because you can make them in pretty color palettes.

▲ Two wire heart links form the center of this figure-8 link bracelet. I also connected the hearts through the center loops with figure-8 links. I used an exaggerated hook to complete the bracelet look. See p. 48 for wire heart instructions.

simple figure-8 clasp

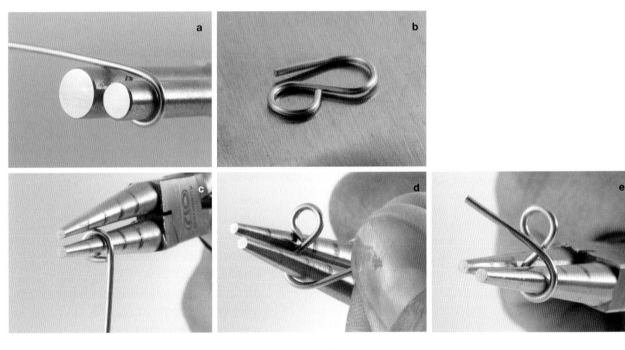

Hook

1 Flush cut a 2¼-in. piece of 16-gauge round wire. Using a 6mm mandrel or 6mm bail-maker pliers, make a simple loop at one end of the wire **a**.

2 Using a 8mm mandrel or bail-making pliers, place the simple loop on the pliers and wrap the wire around the pliers until the wire touches the top of the simple loop.

3 Trim the excess so that the trim is even to the middle of the first loop **b**. Gently hammer the whole piece, and because wire spreads as you hammer, reshape it if needed.

Eye

4 Flush cut a 2¼-in. piece of 16-gauge round wire. Using round-nose pliers at the ½-in. plier mark, make a simple loop at one end of the wire **c**.

5 Using roundnose pliers, place the simple loop on the pliers at the ½-in. plier mark and wrap the wire around the pliers until the wire crosses over the center of the wire and past the first loop **d, e**. This will make a figure-8 shape.

6 Trim the excess so that the trim is flush and touching the center of the wire. Gently hammer the whole piece and because wire spreads as you hammer, reshape it if needed.

top drilled woven bezel pendant

This woven bezel is a unique way to not only encase a beautiful stone like this lapis lazuli, but to also show off beautiful wire weaving. It is easily adaptable to use almost any weave pattern and thickness of stone simply by increasing the number of base wires and changing weave patterns.

: materials

- 3½-in. circumference teardrop shaped top-drilled bead
- 42-in. piece of 20-gauge round wire
- 144-in. piece of 28-gauge round wire on bobbin
- 9 2mm round large hole copper beads

: tools

- long-tined roundnose pliers
- 8mm bail-making pliers or mandrel
- flatnose pliers
- chainnose pliers
- flush cutters
- small file or wire rounder
- permanent marker
- ruler
- polishing cloth

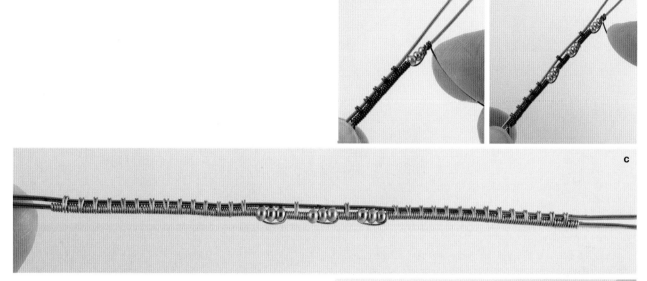

1 Flush cut two 14-in. and one 12-in. pieces of 20-gauge round wire. Line up the 14-in. wires flat and flush and place tape at one end to hold them in place. Mark the center of the two wires and then mark 1¾-in. on each side of the center mark. The area between these marks becomes the woven bezel around the stone.

2 To make it easier to see, I have used purple weave wire. Start this version of Weave 1 (p. 90) with five coils on the base wire 1 (bottom wire). Complete two wraps completely around base wires 1 and 2 and then back to five more coils around base wire 1. Continue this pattern until you have five complete weave rotations. Finish the weave with four coils around base wire 1.

3 String three small copper beads onto base wire 1. Weave around the three beads just as you would when making a beaded coil (p. 89). Make four coils on base wire 1 **a**, then two complete wraps around base wires 1 and 2, and then four more coils on base wire 1.

4 Repeat step 3 so you have three sets of three beads woven onto base wires 1 and finished with four coils on base wire 1 **b**.

5 Complete two wraps around base wires 1 and 2 and then back to five coils around base wire 1. Continue this pattern until you again have five complete weave rotations that match the other side. Finish the weave with five coils **c**.

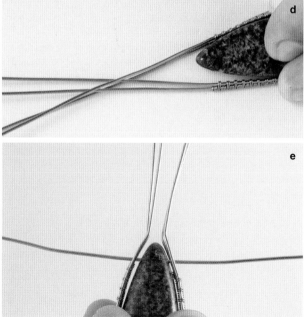

6 Shape the bezel, centering the middle three beads at the bottom center of the stone. The top woven ends of the bezel should also align at the top tip of the stone **d**.

7 With flatnose pliers, make a bend in the top wires so that they are parallel to each other. Center the stone on the 12-in. piece of 20-gauge round wire **e**.

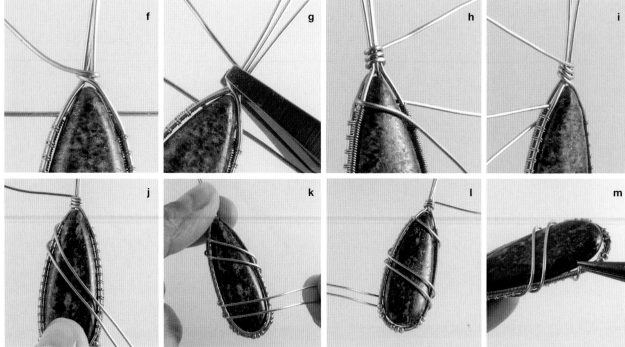

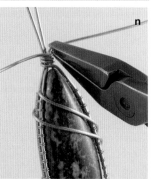

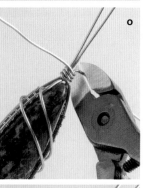

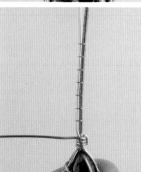

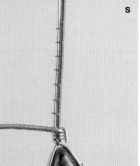

8 Holding the stone so that the front faces you, take the front top wire and wrap it tightly three times around the other three wires **f**. Crimp the wraps tight with flatnose pliers **g**. These three base wraps will make the base of the bail.

9 Push the side of the 12-in. centered wire that is on the same side as the wire wrapped in step 8 around the back of the stone **h** and out to the same side as the other half of the 12-in. wire **i**. Bring both ends of this wire around and across the front of the stone **j**. Wrap both wires together, around the back of the stone, and again across the front of the stone **k**.

10 You can see the two long wire ends sticking out from the back of the stone **l**. Flush cut these wires ½ in. from the side of the stone. You will use these ends to tuck into the back of the bezel edge.

11 With chainnose pliers, put a slight bend in the wire tips and tuck the wire between the bezel and the stone at the back **m**. Carefully crimp these wires down tight against the bezel. (Alternatively, you could leave more wire in step 10, pull them through, and make tiny spirals along the side of the bezel.)

12 Use flatnose pliers to bend the wire that is across from the wrapped wire at a 90-degree angle **n**. Flush cut this wire the length of the three base wraps **o** and crimp the wire to the side of the wraps. This leaves two top wires for the bail and one side wire for wrapping around the base of the bail **p**.

13 Using the two bail wires, start Weave 7 (p. 92) above the wraps with 10 coils on base wire 1 **q** (purple wire used for visibility). Follow the pattern and complete seven complete weave rotations.

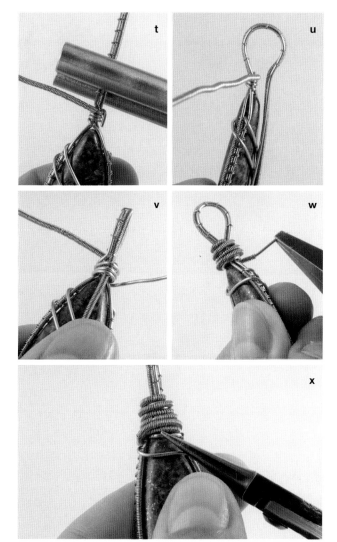

14 Coil along the wire stopping about 1 in. from the end of the wire on base wire 1 **r**.

15 Coil on the wire that is at a 90-degree angle to the side of the stone, leaving about 1 in. uncoiled at the end **s**.

16 Using a 8mm mandrel or bail-making pliers, bend the two bail wires about ¼-in. from the top of the base wraps **t** around the 8mm pliers side and to the front of the pendant **u**.

17 With flatnose pliers, use the uncoiled wire at the front to wrap tightly around the base of the bail from top to bottom **v**. Tuck this wire in (p. 14).

18 Use the coiled wire at a 90-degree angle to the pendant to continue wrapping around the base **w**. Tuck this wire in.

19 Use the coiled wire on the front and continue to wrap around the base. Tuck in the tail.

20 Add patina, if desired, following manufacturer's instructions.

more ideas

◀ This Tiffany stone pendant had a thick edge and needed a three-weave bezel. I used three base wires and coiled beads with loops and tiny spirals to create this look.

▶ The color of this banded agate stone looks fabulous with a copper woven bezel. I used a three-wire base with a variation on Weave 5.

◀ This chrysocola pendant also looks beautiful woven in copper. I used a thick and random bezel weave, a single-coiled wire bail, and a large accent-woven spiral on the front.

▶ This lapis lazuli pendant follows the project directions, but the beaded coiled wire and spiral on the front of the pendant are slightly different.

elegant cotter pin chain

The cotter pin chain is a very old chain design. I love to use this chain link for earring components, in bracelets, or as components in other types of chain projects.

: materials

- 72-in. piece of 18-gauge round wire
- **2** 6mm outer diameter 18-gauge open round jump rings
- 8mm outer diameter 16-gauge open round jump ring

: tools

- long-tined roundnose pliers
- 6mm bail-making pliers or mandrel
- flatnose pliers
- chainnose pliers
- flush cutters
- small file or wire rounder
- chasing hammer
- bench block
- permanent marker
- ruler
- polishing cloth

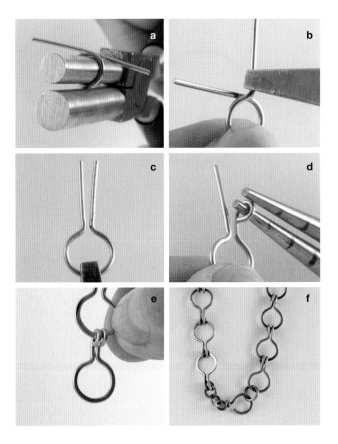

1 Flush cut a 2-in. piece of 18-gauge round wire. Mark ½-in. from each end and in the center of the wire.

2 Using 6mm bail-making pliers, at the center wire mark, center the wire on the plier and loop both sides of the wire around the plier until it crosses over and past each end. The ½-in. marks should be touching **a**.

3 Use flatnose pliers to bend the two end wires parallel to each other at the ½-in. wire marks. The bends should also be perpendicular to the loop **b, c**.

4 Using roundnose pliers, make a simple loop on the ¼-in. plier mark at each end of the wire. The loops should be facing the same direction **d**.

5 Using flatnose pliers, squeeze the two simple loops together until they are touching.

6 Gently hammer the curve of the larger loop and reshape if needed.

7 Repeat steps 1–3. At one end of the wire, make a simple loop on the ¼-in. plier mark. Repeat step 6.

8 Feed the straight end of the wire through the simple loops of the first link. Complete the last simple loop at the end of the wire **e**.

9 Repeat step 5. You have now connected two of the chain's links. Make a total of 34 connected links.

more ideas

◀ These whimsical earrings were made by using larger cotter pin links. I strung beads and ovals onto the wire before making the last simple loop in the link.

I used some striking orange enameled copper focal beads and a connector bail to create this cotter pin and orange beaded necklace.

◀ Combining beads and cotter pin links makes a beautiful bracelet. Use beads to custom colorize your bracelets to your wardrobe.

10 Flush cut a 2-in. piece of 18-gauge round wire. Using 6mm bail-making pliers, make the hook of a wrapped-loop clasp (p. 34).

11 Attach the 8mm 16-gauge jump ring to one end of the chain. Attach the hook to the chain with the two 6mm jump rings **f**.

12 Add patina, if desired, following manufacturer's instructions.

wrapped loop clasp

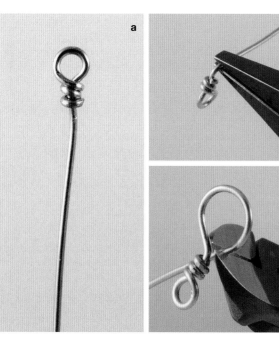

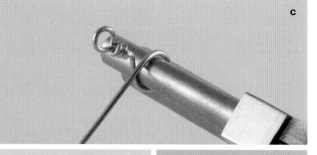

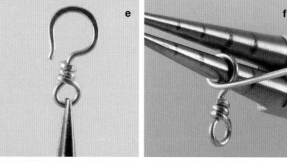

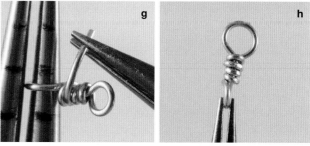

Hook

1 Flush cut a 3-in. piece of 18-gauge round wire. Using roundnose pliers at the ¼-in. plier mark, make a wrapped loop at one end **a**.

2 Using flatnose pliers, bend the wire perpendicular and to the side of the loop **b**.

3 Using the 8mm side of the bail-making pliers, wrap the wire around the pliers to make the hook **c**. Trim even with the wrapped loop **d**.

4 With flatnose pliers, make a small bend at the tip of the hook. Gently hammer all but the wrapped loop **e**.

Eye

5 Flush cut a 3-in. piece of 18-gauge round wire. Using roundnose pliers at the ¼-in. plier mark, make a wrapped loop at one end of the wire.

6 Repeat step 2 of "hook."

7 Using roundnose pliers at the ½-in. mark, make a wrapped loop **f, g**.

8 Trim the excess and gently hammer the curves of the loops **h**.

spiraled s-hook clasp

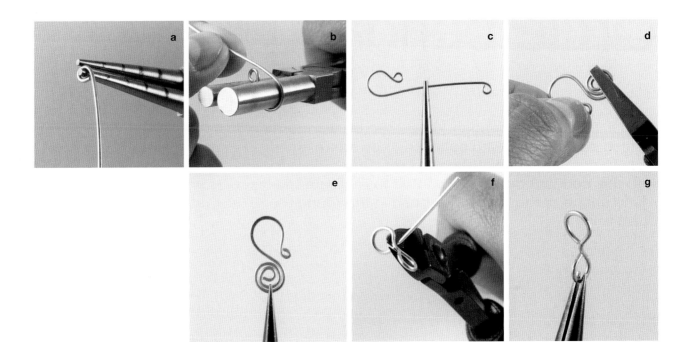

Hook

1 Flush cut a 3½-in. piece of 18-gauge round wire. Using round-nose pliers at the ¼-in. plier mark, make a simple loop at one end of the wire **a**.

2 Using the 8mm side of the bail-making pliers, grasp the wire above the simple loop and wrap the wire around the pliers until the wire touches the top of the loop **b**.

3 At the other end of the wire, make a simple loop facing the opposite direction of the first **c**. Spiral the wire until the spiral is even and across from the first loop **d**.

4 Trim the first loop in half with a flush cut, and squeeze the cut wire together with flatnose pliers to make a very tiny loop **e**.

5 Gently hammer the whole piece and because wire spreads as you hammer, reshape it, if needed.

Eye

6 Cut a 2½-in. piece of 18-gauge round wire. Using roundnose pliers at the ¾-in. plier mark, make an eye loop (p. 14) at one end of the wire.

7 Using roundnose pliers at the 1-in. plier mark, make an eye loop perpendicular to the first. Trim any excess wire **f**.

8 Gently hammer the curved ends of each eye loop and because wire spreads as you hammer, reshape and reclose the eye loops, if needed **g**.

front drilled onyx circle pendant

Simple, front-drilled pendant drops can be wonderful fashion statements. With patience, they are relatively easy to create and enjoy. I paired the cotter pin link with this pendant because I wanted to replicate the round shape of the large onyx bead in the round chain link.

: materials

- 30mm diameter round large hole front-drilled pendant
- 7-in. piece of 16-gauge round wire
- 76-in. piece of 18-gauge round wire
- 14-in. piece of 28-gauge round wire
- 14 6mm outer diameter 18-gauge open jump rings

: tools

- long-tined roundnose pliers
- 6mm bail-making pliers or mandrel
- flatnose pliers
- chainnose pliers
- flush cutters
- small file or wire rounder
- chasing hammer
- bench block
- permanent marker
- ruler
- polishing cloth

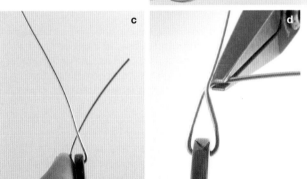

1 Using 18-gauge round wire, follow steps 1–6 of the Elegant Cotter Pin Chain (p. 32). Make a total of 24 links.

2 Flush cut a 1½-in. piece of 18-gauge round wire. Using roundnose pliers at the ½-in. plier mark, make a simple loop at one end.

3 Using roundnose pliers at the ½-in. plier mark, grasp the wire above the loop and wrap it around until it crosses the center of the wire and past the first loop **a** to make a figure-8 shape. Trim the excess wire flush so it is touching the center of the wire. Use flatnose pliers to make sure the wire ends are flush with the center. Gently hammer the link and because wire spreads as you hammer, reshape it if needed. Make 13 of these links.

4 Open a figure-8 link, connect the curved end of a cotter pin link, and close the figure-8 link. Repeat with the other side of the figure-8 link and a second cotter pin link. Use jump rings to connect the loop side of a cotter pin link with the loop side of another cotter pin link **b**. Make two strands of six sets.

5 Attach a figure-8 link to one chain end. Make a wrapped-loop hook (p. 34) and attach it to the other chain end with a jump ring.

6 Flush cut a 6-in. piece of 18-gauge round wire. String the bead on the wire, and leave almost 2 in. of wire at the front and almost 4 in. of wire at the back. Bend these wires up and tight against the bead. Cross the wires **c**.

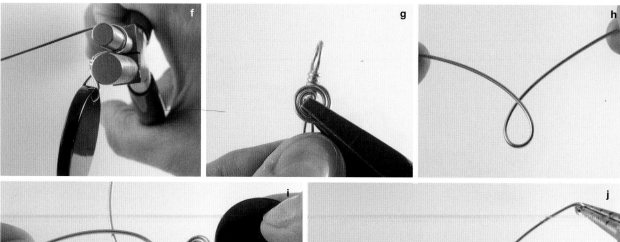

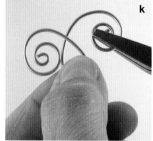

template

note The pendant normally attached on the center loop in photos j–n has been left off so the weaving of the connector bail can be easily illustrated.

7 With flatnose pliers, bend the shorter wire back until it is at a 90-degree angle to the other wire **d**. Make a wrapped loop around the longer wire with the shorter wire. Trim any excess wire.

8 With flatnose pliers, make a 90-degree bend above the wrapped loop and towards the front of the pendant **e**. Using 6mm bail-making pliers, make a wrapped loop **f**. Do not trim this wire. Continue to bring this wire around to the side of the pendant and make a spiral **g**. Position the spiral centered on the front of the pendant.

9 Flush cut a 7-in. piece of 16-gauge round wire. To make the bail, refer to the **template** and follow steps 9 and 10. Mark the center and make a loop by crossing over the wires and pulling the opposite directions **h**. String the pendant onto this loop **i**. Alternatively, you can connect it to a competed connector with a jump ring.

10 With roundnose pliers at the ¼-in. plier mark, make a simple loop at each end of the wire **j**. With flatnose pliers, make an open spiral on each side of the wire **k**.

11 Using the 14-in. 28-gauge round wire, coil four times around the spiral edge, wrap five times around the spiral and loop wires together, and then continue to coil around the loop wire until you reach the two center wires **l**. Make two wraps around the two center wires **m**, and continue coiling until you reach the other spiral edge side. Wrap five times around the loop and spiral edge wires, and finish with four coils around the spiral edge wire **n**. Trim the extra wire.

12 Attach the pendant and bail to the chain with jump rings. Be sure that the cotter pin links are attached going the same direction with the simple loops facing the same direction.

13 Add patina, if desired, following manufacturer's instructions.

more ideas

◀ I found this dalmatian stone bead to be interestingly spotted so I made a large upside-down spiral for a bail and a graduated cotter pin chain. I attached an oval jump ring chain to complete the look.

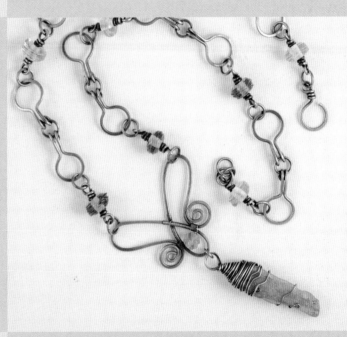

▶ I love the look of a natural stone and forest colors. So, for this alternative, I used a natural, unpolished, top-drilled green kyanite bead, exaggerated the bail, and added different hues of green lampworked beads to make a necklace reminiscent of a cool, shaded forest.

◀ I have had this fall colored flower lampworked pendant for quite a while. One day I was making very round cotter pin links, and it came to me that the link would mimic the shape of my pendant beautifully.

loop on loop chain

This chain is not only versatile, but it is also strong and can hold heavy stones and pendants. Make large heavy-gauge links, graduated links, or mix in other links and components for completely different looks.

: materials

- 72-in. piece of 18-gauge round wire
- **32** 6mm outer diameter 18-gauge open round jump rings

: tools

- long-tined roundnose pliers
- 6mm bail-making pliers or mandrel
- flatnose pliers
- chainnose pliers
- small file or wire rounder
- flush cutters
- chasing hammer
- bench block
- permanent marker
- ruler
- polishing cloth

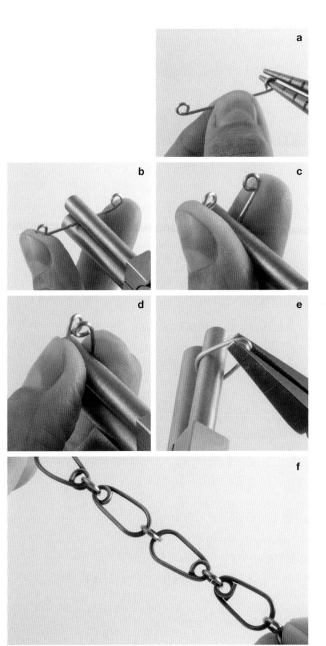

1 Flush cut a 2-in. piece of 18-gauge round wire and mark the center of the wire.

2 At the ¼-in. roundnose plier mark, make a simple loop at each end of the wire. Make the loops on the same side of the wire **a**.

3 With 6mm bail-making pliers, center the wire on the plier at the center wire mark **b**, and push the loops around the plier **c** until they are even and across from each other **d**.

4 Squeeze the loops together with flatnose pliers so that they are touching each other **e**. Remove the link from the pliers and reshape with flatnose pliers, if needed. Hammer the curved portion of the link. Make 32 links.

5 Connect all the links with jump rings **f**.

6 Flush cut a 3-in. piece of 18-gauge round wire. Using roundnose pliers on the ¼-in. plier mark, make a wrapped loop at one end of the wire.

7 Mark ¾ in. from the other end of the wire. With roundnose pliers, make a small, simple loop at the tip of the wire at this end.

8 Center the 6mm bail-making pliers on the mark and make a curve. The tip of the small, simple loop should be even with the top of the wrapped loop. Flush cut the small, simple loop in half and re-close the loop with flatnose pliers.

9 Hammer all but the wrapped loop. The shape of this hook should mimic the shape of the chain links. Attach the hook with a 6mm jump ring **g**.

10 Add patina, if desired, following manufacturer's instructions.

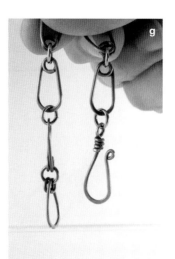

more ideas

◀ For this beautiful necklace, I used double wrapped-loop caged aquamarine beads, sterling silver, and a wrapped, double loop eye.

▶ Tiny gold-filled Loop on Loop links and rutilated quartz beads helped to create a very dressy look for this necklace.

▶ I made jumbo Loop on Loop links and dangled moss agate beads in the center from the loops to create some fun earrings.

◀ Turning the links upside down and then dangling turquoise from the loops gave this earring set a totally unique look.

freeform fun pendant & necklace

The freeform pendant is light and airy. It can either be dressed up with faceted fancy beads and components for a formal look or dressed down for an easy casual look. I have made many of these necklaces with matching earring sets, complete with crystals and pearls for bridal parties and in school colors.

: materials

- 20-in. piece of 16-gauge round wire
- 78-in. piece of 18-gauge round wire
- 21-in. of 26 or 28-gauge round wire for sewing
- **38** 6mm 18-gauge outer diameter round open jump rings
- 8mm 16-gauge outer diameter round open jump ring
- **18** 6mm round beads
- **3** 4mm round beads
- **3** heavy-gauge 3-in. headpins

: tools

- long-tined roundnose pliers
- 6mm bail-making pliers or mandrel
- flatnose pliers
- chainnose pliers
- flush cutters
- small file or wire rounder
- chasing hammer
- bench block
- permanent marker
- ruler
- polishing cloth

43

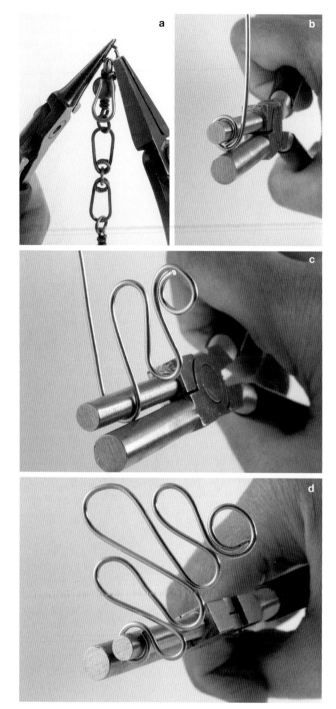

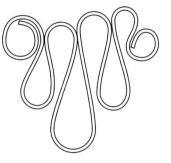

template

1 Follow steps 1–6 of the Loop-on-Loop chain (p. 40). Make 20 links. Connect these links with jump rings so that the simple loops face across from each other. This will make 10 components.

2 Using a 2½-in. piece of 18-gauge round wire and the 6mm round beads, make 12 double wrapped-loop caged beads (p. 13).

3 Use jump rings to connect the double wrapped loop beads between each loop-on-loop component **a**.

4 Flush cut a 3-in. piece of 18-gauge round wire and make a wrapped loop hook (p. 34)

5 Attach the hook to the end of one end of the chain with a 6mm jump ring. Attach the 8mm 16-gauge jump ring to the other end of the chain end as an eye.

6 Flush cut a 20-in. piece of 16-gauge round wire. Using the 6mm bail-making pliers, make a loop at one end of the wire **b**.

7 About 1 in. down from the center of the loop, using the 6mm bail-making pliers, make a curve. Follow with six more curves alternating in a freeform manner between the 6mm bail-making pliers and the 8mm **c**.

8 Finish the pendant frame with a loop made on the 6mm bail-making pliers **d**. (See **template** above.)

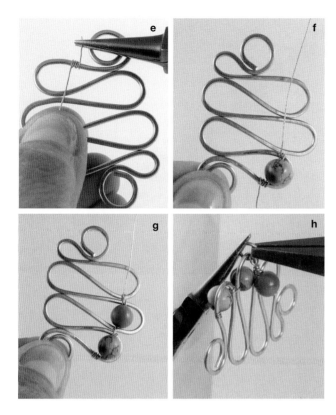

9 Hammer the whole frame evenly with the chasing hammer. Reshape the frame.

10 Using the 28-gauge round wire, randomly sew the 6mm and 4mm round beads on the frame (p. 12) **e**, **f**, **g**.

11 Using three 6mm round beads and the three headpins, make three wrapped loop beads (p. 13). Using three jump rings, attach the wrapped loop beads to the frame **h**.

12 Attach the chain to the frame using two jump rings for each side.

13 Add patina, if desired, following manufacturer's instructions.

◀ Making three loops with the bail-making pliers, adding texture with the texture hammer, and wrapping them onto a wrapped loop drop creates some very fun earrings.

▶ Making four Loop on Loop links and attaching two each with jump rings creates the perfect space to sew in beads for some beautiful dainty earrings.

◀ Elongating the loops and adding two different layers of wire and beads adds depth to this design alternative.

▶ For a dramatic look, use a large-gauge wire for the loops, sew in larger faceted beads and pearls, and add accent wire. Attach the pendant to a heavy gauge Loop-on-Loop chain.

coiled half round chain

The coils on this chain are fun and playful, yet very sturdy. I love mixing these coiled links with so many other kinds of chain and projects. I have even used them to create an outer frame for a suspended frame pendant.

: materials

- 84-in. piece of 12-gauge half-round wire
- 10-in. piece of 16-gauge round wire
- **34** 8mm outer diameter 16-gauge open round jump rings

: tools

- long-tined roundnose pliers
- 6mm/8mm bail-making pliers or mandrels
- flatnose pliers
- chainnose pliers
- flush cutters
- small file or wire rounder
- chasing hammer
- bench block
- permanent marker
- ruler
- polishing cloth

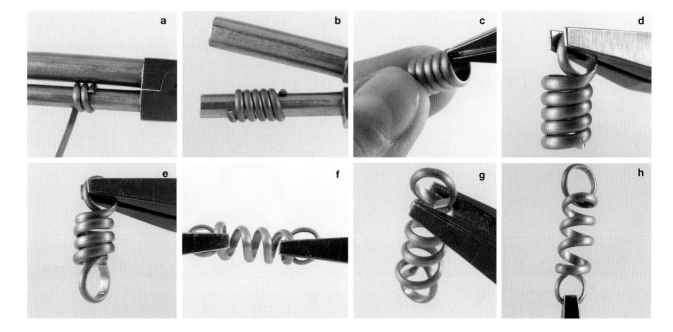

1 Using the concave side of the flush cutters, cut a 5-in. piece of 12-gauge half-round wire. This will create a beveled edge on the wire end so that it will transition better on the link. Do this for both ends of the wire.

2 Using the 6mm bail-making pliers, place the flat side of the half-round wire against the plier jaw and wrap the wire around the jaw from end of wire to end of wire **a**, **b**.

3 Using flatnose pliers, lift and bend up each end of the link to make closed curved loops at the ends **c**, **d**, **e**.

4 Use flatnose pliers to grasp the last wrap on each side of the link and stretch evenly by gently pulling apart with the pliers **f**.

5 With flatnose pliers, center the looped ends of the links by gently squeezing the last coil to position the loop in the center of the last coil **g**, **h**. Make 16 links.

6 Connect each link with two jump rings. This will better match the loop ends and make for a more substantial looking necklace.

7 Make a heart clasp (p. 48). Attach a clasp half to each necklace half with jump rings.

more ideas

▲ I wanted to have a little more color in my bracelet, so I added beads within each link, as well as between each link.

► I made earring drops by using two of the links and adding bead drops to the bottom of each.

▲ Sterling silver, caged onyx beads and a wrapped clasp make this necklace a stand out.

heart clasp

Hook

1 Flush cut a 4-in. piece of 16-gauge round wire. Follow these instructions and use the **templates** (below) as a guide. Mark 1¼ in. from one end of the wire. Using roundnose pliers, on the ¼-in. plier mark, make a wrapped loop on the wire mark.

2 Using a 6mm mandrel or bail-making pliers, make a curve or three-quarter loop on each side of the mark crossing the wire ends at the bottom (**a**, **b**, **c**). Squeeze the center together with flatnose pliers.

3 Trim the wire even with the loop **d**. Make a small loop at the end of the wire and pinch it together with flatnose pliers **e**, **f**.

4 Add patina, if desired, following manufacturer's instructions.

templates

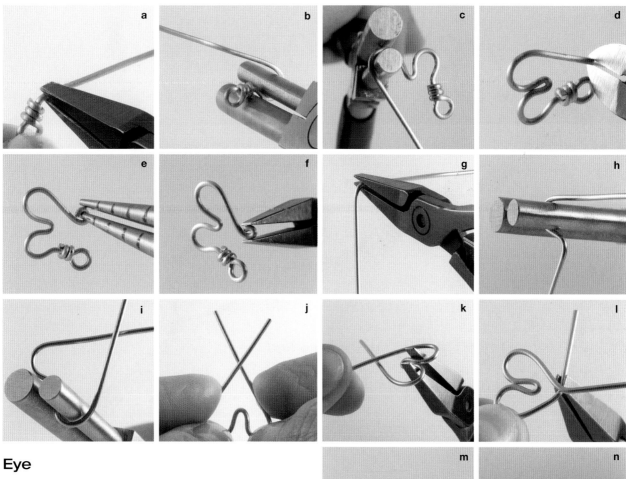

Eye

5 Flush cut a 4-in. piece of 16-gauge round wire. Follow these instructions and use the **templates** (p. 48). Mark the center.

6 Using flatnose pliers, make a 90-degree bend on the wire mark **g**.

7 Using a 6mm mandrel or bail-making pliers, make a curve or three-quarter loop on each side of the mark. Cross the wire ends **h**, **i**, **j**.

8 Using flatnose pliers, squeeze the center heart wires until they are touching **k**.

9 Using flatnose pliers, bend the end wires at a 90-degree angle **l**.

10 Wrap the tail around the stem **m**. Use your fingers and pliers to better shape your heart. Make an eye loop with the remaining wire **n**. Trim any excess wire. Gently hammer all but the wrapped wires.

11 Add patina, if desired, following manufacturer's instructions.

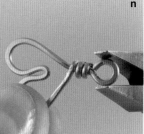

hearts fancy woven bead drop

A heart-shaped centerpiece and clasp unify this fanciful chain and pendant combination.

: materials

- 26-in. piece of 12-gauge half-round wire
- 6-in. piece of 16-gauge round wire
- 74-in. piece of 18-gauge round wire
- 72-in. piece of 28-gauge round wire
- **13** 12mm organic shaped large-hole faceted beads
- **62** 8mm outer diameter 16-gauge round open jump rings
- 18-gauge 6mm outer diameter open jump ring
- 3-in. heavy-gauge headpin

: tools

- long-tined roundnose pliers
- 6mm and 8mm bail-making pliers or mandrels
- flatnose pliers
- chainnose pliers
- flush cutters
- small file or wire rounder
- chasing hammer
- bench block
- permanent marker
- ruler
- polishing cloth

Pendant

1 Flush cut two 10-in. pieces of 18-gauge round wire. Mark the center of each wire. On one wire make a 90-degree bend on the mark. On the other wire, make a loop using the ¼-in. plier mark on roundnose pliers **a**.

2 Mark 1¼-in. on each side of the center mark. Hold the two wires together so that the looped wire is on the outside of the bent wire and they are center point to center point. The bent wire is base wire 1 and the looped wire is base wire 2.

3 Start a Weave 1 (p. 90) alternative with 10 coils on base wire 1 then three wraps on base wires 1 and 2 **b**. Make five complete weave rotations ending in 10 coils on base wire 1 and finishing with eight two-wire wraps to the center.

4 Start the next side with eight two-wire wraps and then 10 coils on base wire 1. Follow these coils with five complete weave rotations to match the other side **c**. Weave 20 coils on base wire 1 followed by three two-wire wraps around base wires 1 and 2. Complete four weave rotations ending with twenty coils on base wire 1.

5 Use your fingers to give the frame a drop shape where the top four wires cross over each other at the end of the shortest weave pattern **d**.

6 Bend the two wires with the shortest weave pattern 90 degrees out to the side and bend the longest weave wire over and behind to the back of the pendant crossing back onto itself on the side and where the weave ends **e**. Holding the frame from the top, take the wire with the coiled end and go around the front and feed it through the center and across the back of the frame at the bottom. Wrap this wire two times around the frame and then make a small spiral and crimp it to the frame with flatnose pliers **f, g**.

7 Bring the second wire around to the front **h** and string two 12mm beads on the wire. With chainnose pliers, wrap the rest of this wire around the top of the frame and make a small spiral at the end **i**. Crimp down this spiral to the frame with flatnose pliers.

8 Use flatnose pliers to bend the two remaining top wires perpendicular to each other **j**. Wrap the side wire around the neck of the top wire and the frame, finishing with one wrap and a small spiral along the side of the frame. Crimp the spiral to the frame with flatnose pliers.

9 Use flatnose pliers to put a slight bend out to the side in the top wire **k**.

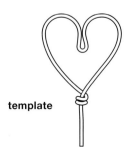

template

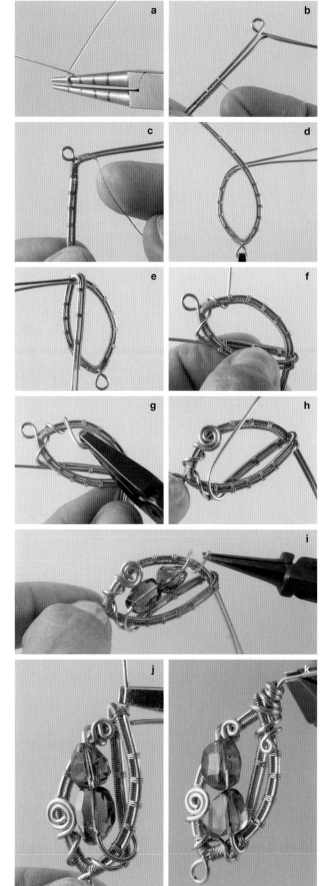

10 Using roundnose pliers at the ½-in. plier mark, make two loops **l**. Wrap the wire around and trim and tuck the tail.

Heart Bail

11 Flush cut a 6-in. piece of 16-gauge round wire. Refer to the **template** (p. 51). Mark the center of the wire. Using flatnose pliers, make a 90-degree bend at the mark. Using an 8mm mandrel or bail-making pliers, make a curve or three-quarter loop on each side of the mark and cross the wire ends. After making the curves, make the center of the heart more pronounced by squeezing it together with flatnose pliers.

more ideas

◀ Turn the Woven Bead Drop frame from a drop into a spiraled heart and add red accent beads.

▶ Here, eliminate the beads, wrap and swirl the wire, and turn the Woven Bead Drop frame upside down for another great look.

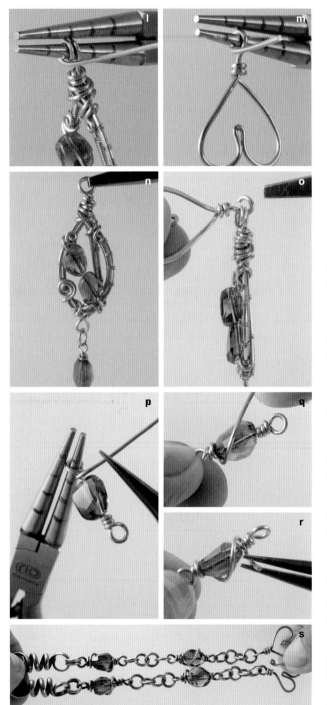

12 Using flatnose pliers, bend the end wires to a 90-degree angle. Wrap the tail wire around the neck. Use your fingers and pliers to better shape your heart.

13 With roundnose pliers, make an eye loop (p. 14) perpendicular to the heart shape **m**. Trim any excess wire. Hammer all but the wrapped wires. This is the connector bail for the pendant.

Finishing

14 With a headpin and a 12mm bead, make a double wrapped-loop caged-link bead (p. 13). Attach the dangle to the pendant with a 6mm jump ring **n**.

15 Open the eye loop at the bottom of the bail with flatnose pliers and attach the pendant. Close the eye loop **o**. Keep the opening of the eye loop on the same side as the back of the pendant.

16 Flush cut 10 5-in. pieces of 18-gauge round wire. Make a double wrapped-loop caged-bead link (p. 13) using roundnose pliers at the ¼-in. mark and a 12mm bead. Make 10 **p**, **q**, **r**.

17 Flush cut six 4-in. pieces of 12-gauge half-round wire. Using a 6mm mandrel, follow steps 1–5 of the coiled half-round chain (p. 46). Make six links.

18 Using flatnose pliers and two 8mm jump rings each, attach a bead link to each side of the heart bail. Using two jump rings each, attach a half-round chain link to each of the bead links. Continue this pattern until you have used three chain links on each side of the chain and four bead links on each side of the chain.

19 Connect four 8mm jump rings, a wrapped bead link, and four jump rings to each end of the chain. Attach the heart clasp to the last jump ring on each end of the chain **s**.

20 Add patina, if desired, following manufacturer's instructions.

double thick wrapped loop clasp

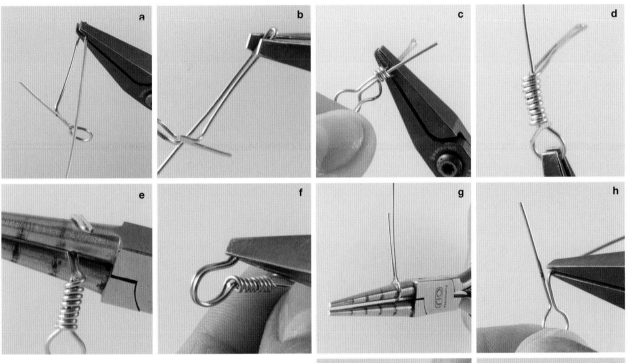

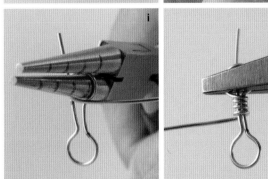

Hook

1 Flush cut a 7-in. piece of 20-gauge round wire. Mark 1½ in. from one end. Using roundnose pliers at the 1-in. plier mark, grasp the wire at the mark and make a single loop.

2 Leaving the loop on the pliers, use flatnose pliers to bend the loop wire up and parallel with the other wire end. On the longer of the two parallel wires, make a mark ¼-in. from the bends. At this new mark, bend the marked wire out to the side **a**.

3 Make a mark 1 in. from the new bend. At this new mark, using flatnose pliers, bend this wire in half and back on to itself, pressing the wires together **b**.

4 Wrap this wire around both wires back to the top of the loop **c**, **d**. Trim any excess wire.

5 Using a 5mm mandrel or the 1-in. mark on roundnose pliers, make a hooked loop with the doubled wires so that the tip is even with the top of the first loop **e**. Using flatnose pliers, put a slight bend in the tip of the hook **f**. Hammer only the first loop curve.

Eye

6 Flush cut a 6-in. piece of 20-gauge round wire. Repeat Hook steps 1 and 2 **g**, **h**.

7 Using roundnose pliers, make a loop at the 1-in. mark on the pliers at the bend in the wire **i**. Using flatnose pliers to hold the link, use the chainnose pliers to wrap the tail of the wire around both wires back to the other loop **j**. Trim both wire tail ends. Gently hammer the curved loops at each end.

super wrapped loop chain

This chain lives up to its name. It is lightweight, yet very sturdy and easily adapted for different size link applications and wire gauges.

: materials

- 152-in. piece of 20-gauge round wire
- **24** 7mm outer diameter 18-gauge open jump rings

: tools

- long-tined roundnose pliers
- 6mm bail-making pliers or mandrel
- flatnose pliers
- chainnose pliers
- flush cutters
- small file or wire rounder
- chasing hammer
- bench block
- permanent marker
- ruler
- polishing cloth

1 Flush cut a 6-in. piece of 20-gauge round wire. Follow Eye instructions (p. 53) and make 23 links.

2 Follow Hook instructions (p. 53) and make one hook.

3 Attach all the links and the hook with the jump rings. On the end of the chain opposite the hook, add a final jump ring as the eye.

4 Add patina, if desired, following manufacturer's instructions.

more ideas

◀ This chain is a wonderful complement to almost any kind of pendant, such as this green turquoise, woven focal-bead pendant.

Make a fun bracelet by adding wrapped and caged beads.

▶ I made a small top loop and a large bottom loop and strung lampworked beads onto the bottom loop for stunning dangle earrings.

focal bead pendant

I've collected lots of beautiful beads and while I have used so many of them in my projects, I end up with one or two left over from a strand. This woven frame is ideal for creating beautiful pendants and earrings with those beads. It is also very easy to use any number of weave patterns and frame embellishments for different looks.

: materials

- 31-in. piece of 20-gauge round wire
- 10mm round bead
- 60 in. 28-gauge round wire

: tools

- long-tined roundnose pliers
- 6mm bail-making pliers or mandrel
- flatnose pliers
- chainnose pliers
- flush cutters
- small file or wire rounder
- chasing hammer
- bench block
- permanent marker
- ruler
- polishing cloth
- painters tape

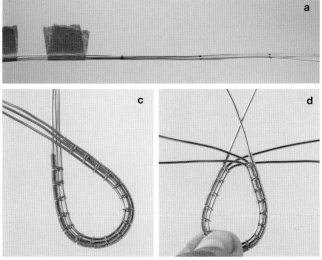

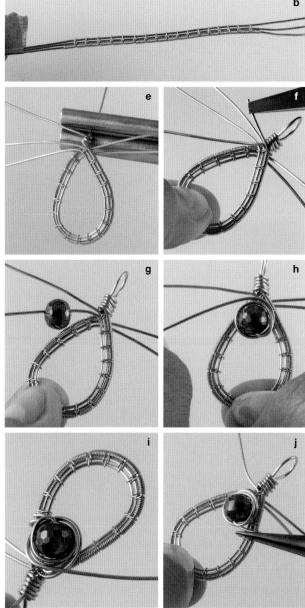

1 Flush cut three 10-in. pieces of 20-gauge round wire. Place the wires side by side, flat and even at the ends. Make a bundle by placing two pieces of painters tape at one end of the wires. Mark the center and 1½ in. on each side of the center mark **a**. Your weave will be between these 1½-in. marks making it very easy to choose different weaves for this frame.

2 Use a variation of Weave 6 (p. 91): Start with base wire 1 and make 10 coils. Wrap base wire 1 and 2 together. Wrap base wires 2 and 3 together carrying the weave wire behind all three wires, and back down and around base wire 1 and 2. Start again with 10 coils on base wire 1 and continue this pattern until you have woven the full distance between the marks, finishing with 10 coils on base wire 1 **b**.

3 Using your fingers, shape your frame into a U-shape with base wire 1 on the outside of the frame. Grasping both ends of the bundle of wires, cross them over each other with the wires on the right side to the front **c**.

4 Bend down the two front bottom wires and the two back bottom wires. This will leave you with two top center wires at the top **d**.

5 Using flatnose pliers, wrap the front center top wire around the base of the back center top wire.

6 Using the 6mm bail-making pliers or mandrel **e**, make a loop bringing the wire down the center of the front of the pendant. With flatnose pliers, use the same wire that you wrapped around the base to wrap around the loop wire about five times to hold it in place **f**. Trim and tuck this wire in at the back.

7 Trim the tail of the loop wire or, as an option, push it to the side and later use it to add spirals to the side of the frame. Lightly hammer only the loop.

8 String a bead on the bottom front wire **g**. Center the bead on the frame and wrap the remainder of the wire around the bead, encircling it **h, i**.

9 Continue with the same wire, bringing it around to the side of the frame and wrapping it around the frame's side. Crimp it down to the frame **j**.

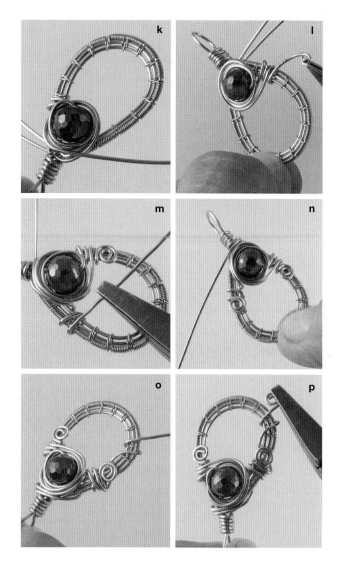

◀ This chrysocola top-drilled bead needed a larger woven frame, so I used 18-gauge round wire and a fuller weave to complement the stone.

▶ This aquamarine druzy had a higher thickness profile, so I used a fuller weave and brought a two-wire weave down the front of the stone to ensure that it would be very secure in the frame.

◀ Weave the bail, add a variety of stones and bead types, then graduate the beads for a dimensional pendant.

▶ Turn the bail wire to the front and make it smaller. Use a large jump ring as the bail, and turn the weave wires inside out. For a more traditional look, use a double loop bail.

10 Grasp the second front wire and encircle the bead twice **k**.

11 Using chainnose pliers, continue with that wire to the side and wrap it around the frame once. Using chainnose pliers, make a small loop at the end of this wire **l**. Using flatnose pliers spiral this end and crimp it to the base.

12 Bring the bottom back wire to the front and around the side of the bead. Using flatnose pliers, wrap this wire two times around the frame **m**. Trim this wire leaving about 1 in. of wire and make a spiral. Use flatnose pliers to crimp the spiral to the frame **n**.

13 Bring the last wire around to the front of the pendant and then around to the back, and wrap it around the frame at the bottom twice **o**. With flatnose pliers, spiral the end **p** and crimp it to the frame. These wires and spirals can be placed any number of ways on the frame.

14 Add patina, if desired, following manufacturer's instructions.

front drilled captured woven pendant

The versatility of this pendant project is fabulous and is by far one of my favorites for front-drilled stones. You can make the project as it is, with weaving or without weaving, or easily change what you weave and where you weave. The step-by-step photos for this pendant are without the weave so that the steps are easy to see. I have also included the weave directions so that you have both options.

: materials

- 40x25mm oval large hole top front drilled stone bead
- 30-in. piece of 20-gauge round wire
- 48 in. 28-gauge round wire

: tools

- long-tined roundnose pliers
- 8mm bail-making pliers or mandrel
- flatnose pliers
- chainnose pliers
- flush cutters
- small file or wire rounder
- permanent marker
- ruler
- polishing cloth
- painters tape

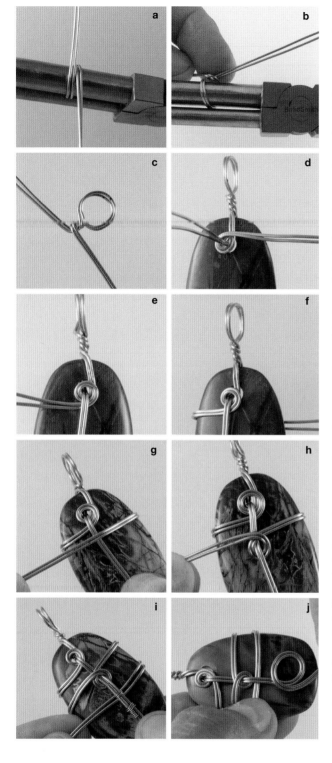

1 Flush cut two 15-in. pieces of 20-gauge round wire. Temporarily tape together the two wires with two flags of painters tape on one side. Measure and mark 9 ½ in. from one end of the wires. Center the 8mm bail-making pliers on the mark and make a loop **a**.

2 Leaving the loop on the pliers, twist the loop two times completely around at the base so that the loop runs in the same direction as the wires **b**, **c**. Crimp the twisted wires together. Remove the tape.

3 String the shorter of the two wire sides through the back of the hole, centering the bail on the top of the stone and pressing the longer front wires against the stone front. Loop the front wires around the wires coming out of the bead hole one time **d**, **e**.

4 Continue with these wires taking them around the back of the stone **f**. Bring these wires across the front of the stone and the other wires again **g**. Loop these wires under and around the other wires **h**.

5 At this point, decide if you wish to add weaving to the pendant and which weave you wish to use. I chose to use an alternative of Weave 1. Start on base wire 1 with twenty coils at the base of your last loop around the front wires. On base wires 1 and 2, make three wraps and return to base wire 1. Repeat this pattern six times. Make 20 coils on base wire 1 followed by two wraps on base wires 1 and 2. Complete four rotations. Finish with 10 coils on base wire 1. Complete all of the weaving on the shorter of the two sets of wires coming from the back.

6 Bring the front wires around the back of the stone to the front, placing them under the woven wires **i**.

7 For illustration purposes, the next photos do not have any woven wires, but are referred to as the woven wires. Make a loop with the woven wires and then trim so that there is about ¾ in. left at the ends **j**, **k**. Splral each end and press them against the stone. You can choose to spiral them in either direction **l**. The weave will make these wires much stiffer and help them stay in place.

8 Lay the front wires back across the woven wires and press them down **m**. Trim the ends to about ¾ in. each. Make a small spiral at each end and press them down against the stone **n**.

9 If the wirework seems a little loose, go to the back of the pendant and place small bends in the wire to tighten the wrappings **o**.

10 Add patina, if desired, following manufacturer's instructions.

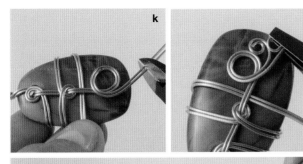

◀ For this variation, I added a lot of weaving and loops to this serpentine pendant for a vintage, machine-works look.

▶ The copper weaving stands out on this native American copper stone. I used three different weave patterns to complete the design.

◀ I went tiny and delicate for this earring variation, turning the top loop to the front and eliminating the weaving.

double loop crossover chain

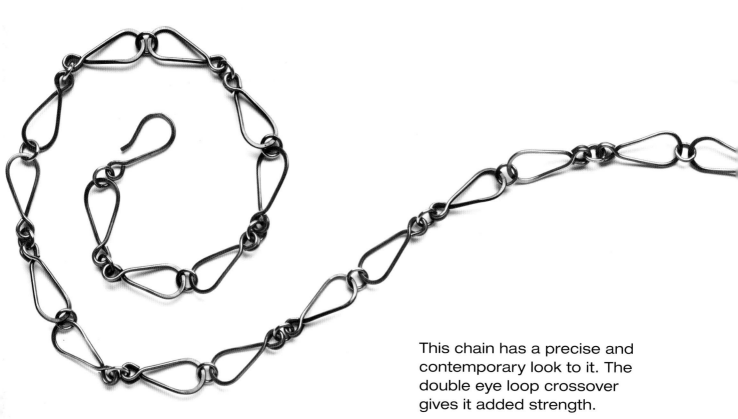

This chain has a precise and contemporary look to it. The double eye loop crossover gives it added strength.

: materials

- 72-in. piece of 16-gauge round wire
- **23** 8mm outer diameter 16-gauge open jump rings

: tools

- long-tined roundnose pliers
- 8mm bail-making pliers or mandrel
- flatnose pliers
- chainnose pliers
- flush cutters
- small file or wire rounder
- chasing hammer
- bench block
- permanent marker
- ruler
- polishing cloth

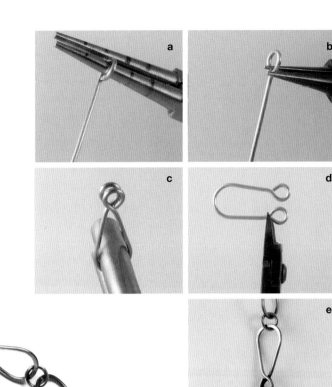

a

b

c

d

e

◀ Sterling silver and caged green kyanite beads highlight this necklace. For simplicity, I used one of the links as the eye of the necklace instead of a jump ring.

Turquoise is one of my favorite stones. This bead is no exception, so I made it the focal point. I made smaller links and made them radiate outward from the stone by lining them up in an eye-to-curve pattern.

◀ These earrings are very dramatic with the woven link-within-link design.

1 Flush cut a 3-in. piece of 16-gauge round wire, and mark the center of the wire. At the ¼-in. roundnose plier mark, make a simple loop at each end of the wire **a**. Make the loops on the same side of the wire.

2 Using chainnose pliers, change the simple loops to eye loops (p. 14) **b**.

3 With the 8mm pliers or mandrel, grasp the wire at the center wire mark and push the loops around the plier until they are even and across from each other.

4 Squeeze the loops together and flat against each other with flatnose pliers **c**. Remove from the pliers and reshape if needed.

5 Hammer the curved portion of the link. Make twenty-three links.

6 Flush cut one eye loop off of one link **d**. Using flatnose pliers, make a small bend on the cut wire end. This creates the hook **e**. Hammer the hook.

7 Connect all the links with jump rings, eye-to-eye and curve-to-curve. Attach the hook to one end with a jump ring. Place a final jump ring on the end opposite the hook to use as the eye.

▶ I love the simplicity of this earring design. The large link and dainty swirls give the earring set a very feminine look. Try using mixed metals with this alternative.

top drilled no frame pendant

This pendant design has the look of a free floating stone because the top-drilled holes can be totally covered with wire and beads so they remain unseen. Just about any top-drilled bead works well with this project.

: materials

- 16-in. piece of 20-gauge round wire
- 72-in. piece 28-gauge round wire
- 10x40mm top-drilled stone

: tools

- long-tined roundnose pliers
- 6mm bail-making pliers or mandrel
- flatnose pliers
- chainnose pliers
- flush cutter
- small file or wire rounder
- permanent marker
- ruler
- polishing cloth

1 Flush cut a 16-in. piece of 20-gauge round wire. String the bead on the wire and center it.

2 Using your fingers, bend each side of the wire up at a 90-degree angle and parallel to each other. Bend each wire across the top of the stone one at a time **a**.

3 Using flatnose pliers, bend up each wire from the center at 90-degree angles and again parallel to each other **b**.

4 I chose to use Weave 7 (p. 92) following the pattern of 10 coils on base wire 1 then one wrap all the way around base wire 2 and back down to base wire 1. To start the weave, make 10 coils on base wire 1 **c**. With the tail of the weave wire, go across both base wires three times. Coil three times around base wire 2 at the base **d**. Trim the tail and crimp it to base wire 2 to secure the weave.

5 Returning to base wire 1, complete 14 rotations of the weave pattern of 10 coils on base wire 1 then one wrap all the way around base wire 2 and back down to base wire 1 **e**. Finish this weave with 10 coils on base wire 1.

6 To start the next coiling pattern, flip the wires over so that base wire 2 becomes base wire 1. Make 10 coils on the new base wire 1 **f**. String a bead onto base wire 1. Coil over the bead and continue this pattern until you have coiled 10 beads **g**. End with 10 wraps.

7 Continuing on the new base wire 1, make 10 coils. Make one complete wrap around base wire 2. Make 20 coils on base wire 1 and one wrap around base wire 2. Make six coils on base wire 1.

8 Measure 1 in. from the wire bends at the base of the weave and place the 6mm bail-making pliers on the wire, centering them on the measurement **h**.

9 Bring these wires over the pliers and to the front of the pendant. Continue to take these wires to the side and back of the other wires **i**.

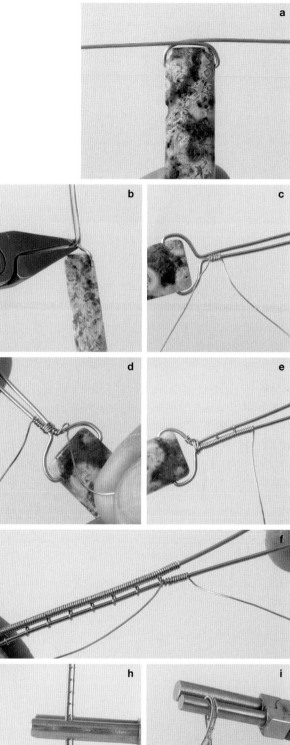

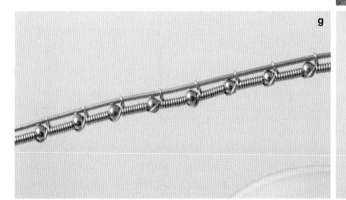

j

k

l

m

10 Wrap these wires around the back and across the front. Make two complete wraps around the wires, bringing the wires down and across the stone at the corner **j**.

11 Continue to wrap the wire around the back of the stone and back across the front of the stone **k**. Wrap around twice ending again at the front of the stone.

12 Flush cut the ends, leaving about ¾ in. of wire out to the side **l**.

13 With flatnose pliers, spiral the two ends and press the spirals to the stone with flatnose pliers **m**.

14 Add patina, if desired, following manufacturer's instructions.

more ideas

◀ I used the Loop on Loop chain with caged aquamarine beads to match this top-drilled aquamarine stone. This shape lends itself well to this project.

▶ I absolutely love the look of this large raw kyanite top-drilled bead. The silver woven bail and wrap really pops with the green of the stone. I further completed this set with a Double Loop Crossover chain and matching kyanite caged beads.

◀ Variscite is one of my favorite green and brown veined stones. The copper weave brings out the brown veining. I added matching coiled crystals to further tie in the stone.

▶ This naturally pink cobalto calcite bead is really stunning with its silver woven bail and wrap.

twisted double loop clasp

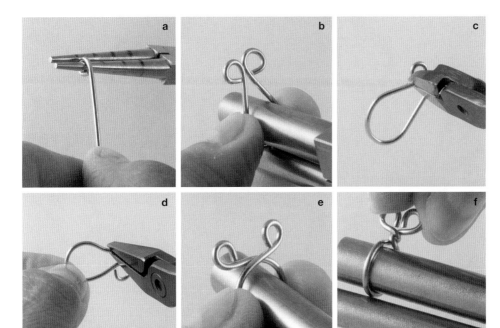

Hook

1 Flush cut a 2¾-in. piece of 16-gauge round wire. Mark the center of the wire.

2 With roundnose pliers, at the ¼-in. plier mark make a simple loop at each end of the wire **a**. The loops should face each other.

3 Using a 10mm mandrel, place the center mark on the mandrel and bend the wire around the mandrel until the loops are side by side and face away from each other **b**.

4 Flush cut away one of the simple loops **c**. With flatnose pliers, make a bend in the hook at the tip **d**. Gently hammer the whole piece and because wire spreads as you hammer, reshape it if needed.

Eye

5 Repeat steps 1 and 2 of Hook.

6 Using the 8mm bail-making pliers, grasp the wire at the center mark and bend the wire around until the loops cross each other. This large loop is the eye **e**.

7 Leaving the large loop on the plier, make a complete twist two times around **f** until the loops are perpendicular to the larger eye loop. Gently hammer everything except where the wire crosses, and reshape it, if needed.

chaplin chain

This chain link is easy to make. The loop-to-loop connection creates an interesting pattern and gives the chain a substantial look.

: materials

- 70-in. piece of 16-gauge round wire
- **32** 8mm outer diameter 16-gauge open round jump rings

: tools

- long-tined roundnose pliers
- 10mm mandrel or bail-making pliers
- 6mm and 8mm bail-making pliers or mandrels
- flatnose pliers
- chainnose pliers
- flush cutter
- small file or wire rounder
- chasing hammer
- bench block
- permanent marker
- ruler
- polishing cloth

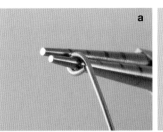
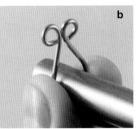
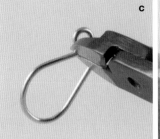

◄ Purple dumortierite double-hole beads adorn this necklace. The double-hole beads line up perfectly with the simple loops of the chain links.

Links

1 Flush cut a 2¾-in. piece of 16-gauge round wire.

2 Using roundnose pliers, make a simple loop at each end of the wire on the ¼-in. mark on the pliers **a**.

3 Using a 10mm mandrel or bail-making pliers, center and wrap the wire around the plier until the edges of the simple loops touch **b**.

4 Remove the link from the mandrel and reshape with flatnose pliers if needed.

5 Hammer the link. Reshape if needed. Make 20.

Hook

6 Repeat "link" steps 1–4.

7 Flush cut away one of the simple loops making a matching hook **c**. With flatnose pliers, make a bend in the hook at the tip **d**, **e**.

8 Gently hammer the whole piece and because wire spreads as you hammer, reshape it if needed.

Eye

9 Make an eye as in steps 5–7 p. 67.

Assemble

10 Assemble the chain loop-to-loop and curve-to-curve using one jump ring through each loop and one jump ring for the curves.

11 With a jump ring, attach the hook to one end and the eye to the other end.

12 Add patina, if desired, following manufacturer's instructions.

▶ The art deco bead fits snugly into the curve of the enlarged link. I added matching dangle beads and a sewn in fresh water pearl.

◄ For this simple and colorful pendant drop, I used a coiling tool to add double-coiled turquoise artistic wire to the enlarged link. I also turned the loops to the side and added a triple-loop bail with jump ring.

▶ These earrings have a touch of sparkle sewn onto the bottom curve of each link.

spiraled front drilled pendant

Red creek jasper is a lovely fall-colored stone and matches beautifully with the patinated copper woven bail and front swirls in this project.

: materials

- 25x40mm front drilled bead with 5mm hole
- 48-in. piece of 20-gauge round wire
- 4-in. piece of 22-gauge round wire
- 36-in. piece of 28-gauge round wire

: tools

- long-tined roundnose pliers
- 6mm bail-making pliers or mandrels
- flatnose pliers
- chainnose pliers
- flush cutter
- small file or wire rounder
- permanent marker
- ruler
- painters tape
- polishing cloth

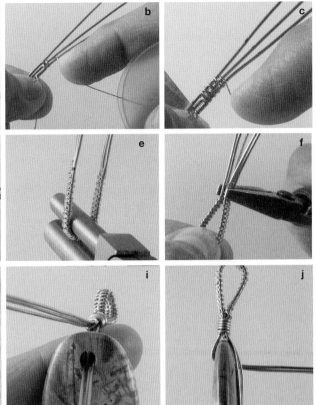

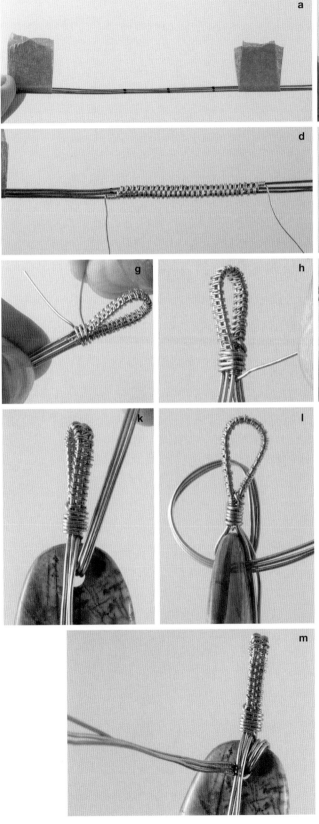

1 Flush cut three pieces 16-in. each of 20-gauge round wire. Tape each end to hold the wires flat. Mark the center and mark ¾-in. on each side of the center mark **a**.

2 Remove one of the pieces of painters tape and weave between the two outside marks for a total of 1½-in. Start the weave with 10 coils on base wire 1. Follow Weave 5 (p. 91), and weave to the end of the 1½-in. section, finishing with 10 coils on base wire 2 **b**, **c**, **d**. Trim the weave tails and crimp to the base wires.

3 Using the 6mm bail-making pliers, center the pliers on the weave. The weave pattern front should be on the outside so that the pattern will be seen and not the back of the pattern. Bend the wire around the pliers, making sure that the weave endings on the base wires are even **e**. This will become the bail.

4 Using flatnose pliers, make a small outward bend on each side of the weave base. Compress the sides together **f**.

5 Using 22-gauge wire, wrap five or six times around the wires at the base of the bail weave **g**. Tuck the top wire end into the bail loop and crimp it down. Tuck the other wire end between the six wires **h**, and crimp it down. Trim the extra wire.

6 String the back three wires through the bead hole and center the bail at the top of the bead. Press the other wires onto the front of the bead **i**, **j**.

7 Pull the back wires toward the top of the stone, around, and back through the hole to the other side of the front wires **k**, **l**. Bring the back wire up toward the top of the stone, around, and back through the hole on the opposite side of the front wires **m**.

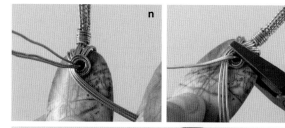

8 Wrap the front wires one full time around the back wires (coming out of the hole) **n**. Press these wires against the stone **o**.

9 Pull both sets of wires at an angle to each other crossing the stone **p**. Trim the wires so that they are each 1¼-in. long, measuring from the center swirl.

10 Using roundnose pliers, at the ¼-in. plier mark, make simple loops at the end of each wire. Face three loops right and three loops left **q**. Spiral each wire end **r**.

11 Using flatnose pliers and press the spirals against the stone.

12 Add patina, if desired, following manufacturer's instructions.

more ideas

▼ Add crystals, change the weave, and use a bright red-dyed stone for a festive pendant.

▼ Forgo the woven bail for a looped bail and add wrapped crystals to a loop topped ceramic bead.

▲ Change the size and color of your stone for a different visual effect. Because of its coloring, this lace stone would look great with copper, silver, or mixed metals.

▲ Choose an unusual shaped stone, such as this onyx triangle. Add swirls to break up the severity and to add softness to the angular shape.

▲ Make a looped bail, add swirls and crystals centering them on a textured ceramic bead, creating a dimensional pendant.

double strength clasp

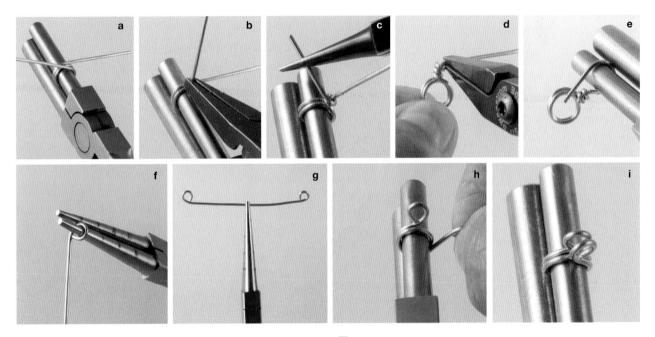

Hook

1 Flush cut a 4-in. piece of 18-gauge round wire. Mark the center of the wire.

2 With 6mm bail-making pliers, make two wraps around the plier, stopping with the wire ends pointing away from each other **a**.

3 With flatnose pliers, bend one of the wires at a 90-degree angle to the other wire **b**. Using chainnose pliers, wrap the extending wire around the neck of the 90-degree wire at least two times **c**. Trim the excess tail.

4 With flatnose pliers, bend the remaining wire parallel to the double loop **d**.

5 Using 8mm bail-making pliers, make a loop for the hook **e**. Trim this wire even with the top of the double loop. Gently hammer the hook and reshape it, if needed.

Eye

6 Flush cut a 2¾-in. piece of 18-gauge round wire. Using round-nose pliers at the ¼-in. plier mark, make facing simple loops at each end of the wire **f, g**.

7 Using the 6mm side of the bail-making pliers, center the wire on the plier and loop the wire around the plier one complete rotation. The loops should face away from the plier upon starting the rotation. Continue the rotation until the simple loops sit across from each other on the pliers **h, i**.

8 Remove the eye from the pliers and reshape with flatnose pliers, if needed.

double strength chain

Of all the projects, this one is my favorite. Not only does this chain look good, it is very strong and easily adaptable.

: materials

- 115-in. piece of 18-gauge round wire
- **38** 6mm outer diameter 18-gauge open round jump rings
- **18** 8mm outer diameter 18-gauge open round jump rings
- 8mm outer diameter 16-gauge open round jump ring

: tools

- long-tined roundnose pliers
- 6mm and 8mm bail-making pliers or mandrels
- 14mm mandrel
- flatnose pliers
- chainnose pliers
- flush cutter
- small file or wire rounder
- chasing hammer
- bench block
- permanent marker
- ruler
- polishing cloth

more ideas

I used the largest of the links to mimic the beautifully textured disk beads. I wrapped the disk beads on top to not only stabilize the beads flat, but to give added visual interest.

◄ These graduated link earrings are fabulous to wear with upswept hair. Try making them with brass, copper, and silver links.

Links

1 Flush cut a 2¾-in. piece of 18-gauge round wire.

2 Follow Eye instructions (p. 73) to make nine links **a**.

3 Flush cut a 3¾-in. piece of 18-gauge round wire.

4 Using roundnose pliers at the 1-in. mark and 8mm bail-making pliers, follow Eye instructions (p. 73) to make eight links.

5 Flush cut a 5-in. piece of 18-gauge round wire.

6 Using roundnose pliers at the 1-in. mark and a 14mm mandrel, follow eye instructions (p. 73) to make 10 links **b**.

Hook

7 Flush cut a 4-in. piece of 18-gauge round wire. With 6mm bail-making pliers, follow Hook instructions (p. 73) to make a hook.

Assemble

8 Attach the links using double 6mm jump rings for the 2¾-in. and 3¾-in. links. Use double 8mm jump rings for the largest of the links. Attach the hook to the side of the necklace that has four 2¾-in. links, and the 16-gauge jump ring to the side with five 2¾-in. links. This will make the necklace even from hook to eye. Refer to the photo, p. 74, for placement.

9 Add patina, if desired, following manufacturer's instructions.

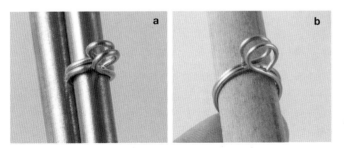

super s
pendant

This woven pendant has simple lines and a contemporary feel. The double strength chain links mixed with the rolo chain further carry the look around the neckline.

: materials

- 8-in. piece of 14-gauge round wire (frame)
- 2½-in. piece of 14-gauge round wire (bail)
- 46-in. piece of 18-gauge round wire
- 45-in. piece of 28-gauge round wire
- **42** 6mm outer diameter open jump rings
- 16-gauge 8mm outer diameter open jump ring
- 16-in. piece of 4.5mm rolo chain

: tools

- long-tined roundnose pliers
- 6mm and 8mm bail-making pliers or mandrel
- 30mm mandrel
- flatnose pliers
- chainnose pliers
- flush cutter
- small file or wire rounder
- chasing hammer
- bench block
- permanent marker
- ruler
- polishing cloth

Pendant

1 Flush cut a 8-in. piece of 14-gauge round wire. Using 6mm bail-making pliers, make a simple loop at one end of the wire **a**.

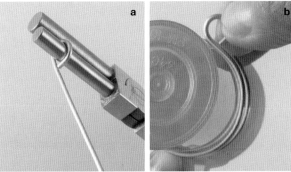

2 Using a 30mm mandrel wrap the wire completely around the mandrel **b, c**.

3 Reshape the frame placing the wire end inside the outer loop.

4 Using roundnose pliers at the ½-in. plier mark, make a simple loop at the end of the inside wire **d**.

5 The weave process for this project is unusual because there is only one circular wire that crosses past itself on which to weave thus making the bobbin unusable. The center wire end becomes base wire 1 and the outer wire edge becomes base wire 2. The weave I chose to use is an adaptation of Weave pattern 8 (p. 92).

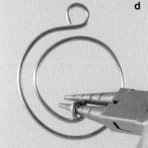
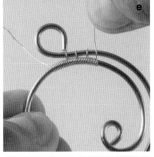

6 Center the inside loop on the frame and start your weave with 10 coils at the point at the top where the wire first crosses past itself. Make one complete wrap around base wire 2 at the tip of the simple loop. Continue with the pattern of 10 coils on base wire 1 and one complete loop around base wire 2 **e** until you are at the end of the inner simple loop. Finish the weave with 10 coils on base wire 2. You could easily substitute almost any weave pattern here.

Bail

7 Flush cut a 2½-in. piece of 14-gauge round wire. Refer to the **template** (below). Using 6mm bail-making pliers, make a simple loop at one end of the wire **f**.

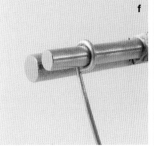

8 Using 8mm bail-making pliers, grasp the wire above the simple loop and wrap the wire around the pliers until the wire crosses the center and extends slightly past the first loop **g**. Trim the excess wire so that the trim is flush and touching the center of the wire. Because of the wire thickness, hammering this figure-8 is optional. Attach the bail to the pendant as you would a jump ring.

template

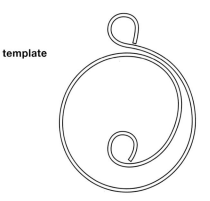

Chain

9 Flush cut a 2¾-in. piece of 18-gauge round wire. Make 12 double-strength eyes (p. 73).

10 Flush cut a 4-in. piece of 18-gauge round wire. With 6mm bail-making pliers for the hook and 8mm bail-making pliers for the loop, make a hook (p. 73).

Assembly

11 Cut the 16-in. rolo chain into five 1¼-in. pieces and two 3¼-in. pieces. Attach all the pieces with double jump rings as shown (p. 76).

12 Place the longest two pieces of rolo chain at the ends. Attach the hook on one end and the 8mm 16-gauge jump ring eye on the other end.

13 Attach the chain links with double jump rings following the pattern shown (photo, p.76).

14 Add patina, if desired, following manufacturer's instructions.

template

more ideas

▲ Create a large figure-8 bail (template, left), eliminate the weave, add a spiral embellishment to one side, and sew in a pearl for a simple soft style.

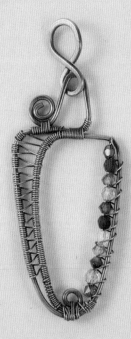

▶ Give the frame a more angled look, add crystal edging, and a woven side for a fun festive pendant.

◀ This project frame can easily be reduced in size to make earrings. Add an amethyst beaded edging and a matching wrapped loop bead dangle for a sassy pair of earrings.

captured serpentine pendant

The beauty of this project is exposing the stone and knowing that it will not fall out of the frame. This serpentine pendant is created from one, large-holed bead and very little wire.

: materials

- 30x25mm large-hole top-drilled bead
- 33-in. piece of 20-gauge round wire
- 60-in. piece of 28-gauge round wire

: tools

- long-tined roundnose pliers
- 8mm bail-making pliers or mandrel
- flatnose pliers
- chainnose pliers
- flush cutter
- small file or wire rounder
- permanent marker
- ruler
- polishing cloth
- painters tape

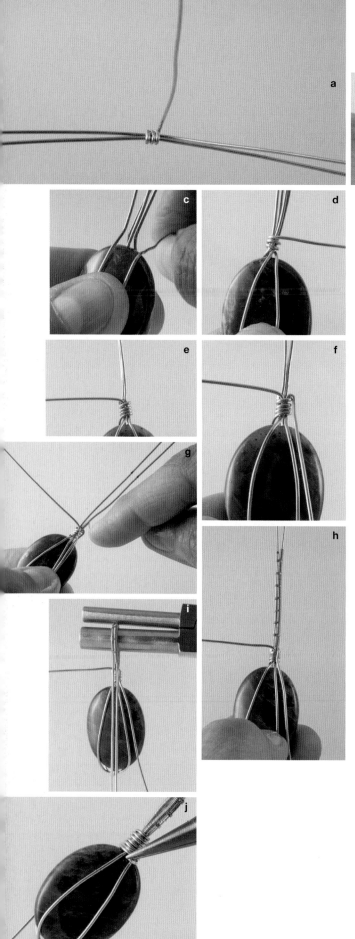

1 Flush cut two 12½-in. and one 7-in. pieces of 20-gauge round wire.

2 Put a piece of painters tape at each end of both 12½-in. wires to temporarily hold them flat and even. Mark the centers of the 12½-in. wires. Wrap the end of the 7-in. piece of 20-gauge round wire, perpendicular and around the center mark of both wires, three times. Crimp the wraps flat with flatnose pliers **a**.

3 String the bead onto the 7-in. wire **b**.

4 Bring the front set of two wires up and to the front of the bead. Bring the back two wires up and against the back of the bead. Using flatnose pliers, squeeze all of the wires at the top.

5 Wrap one of the front wires **c** three times around all of the other wires **d**. This will become the bail base. Trim the excess wire (or, bend this wire down and use it for embellishment in the weave).

6 Bend the remaining front wire to the side at a 90-degree angle **e**.

7 Bend one of the front two wires down to the front and against the bail base **f**. Crimp it close to the base with flatnose pliers.

8 The two wires left at the top become the bail. Mark each wire 1¼ in. from the base and make 10 coils on base wire 1 **g**.

9 Choose your weave pattern (I chose Weave 1, p. 90) and coil 10 on base wire 1, wrap two around both base wires and back to base wire 1, and repeat. Weave for the full 1¼-in. and finish with 10 coils on base wire 1 **h**.

10 Using 8mm bail-making pliers, grasp the bail wires 1-in. from the top of the bead. Loop the wire over the bail-making pliers and onto the front of the pendant **i**.

11 Wrap the wire extending to the side tightly around all of the bail wires. Stop at the bead. Trim and tuck in the tail **j**.

12 Choose a weave pattern (I chose a variation of Weave 6 p. 91) . Start the weave on base wire 1 with 20 coils **k**. As with weave 6, go up from base wire 1, wrap base wire 2, and then from base wire 2 wrap base wire 3, and then all the way back down to base wire 1. Follow this with another wrap from base wire 1 to base wire 2 and then back to base wire 1. Repeat this rotation **l**.

13 Finish with 60 coils on base wire 1. Trim and crimp the tail to base wire 1. Trim and crimp the tail from the start of the weave.

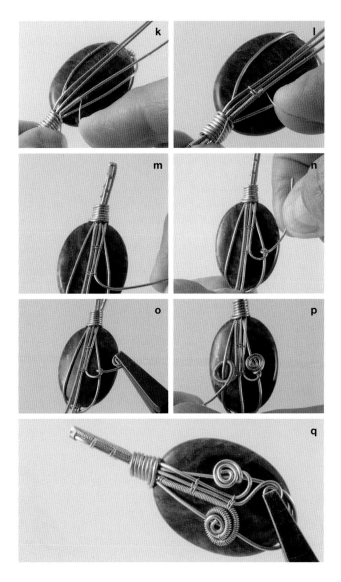

14 With base wire 3, make a curved bend in the wire and direct the tail out to the side of the stone **m**. Wrap the wire once around the wire against the stone and make a small spiral **n**, **o**. Press the spiral to the stone with flatnose pliers.

15 Make a curve in the wire opposite the spiral. Loop the wire under and around the wire against the stone **p**. Make a spiral with flatnose pliers and press it against the stone. Be careful not to hold the wire too tightly in the pliers because the pressure could mar the coils.

16 Make a 90-degree bend in the middle wire. Using flatnose pliers, make a spiral in this wire. Spiral the wire in the opposite direction of the bend **q**.

17 Add patina, if desired, following manufacturer's instructions.

more ideas

◀ Change the bail weave and add more loops and woven spirals on a turquoise bead for an eye-catching style.

▶ For this alternative, I found some lovely Washington State petrified wood and knew I had to wrap it in silver. I added pearls to contrast with the rich, dark, wood grain.

◀ This green Mexican turquoise bead caught my eye at a show and I not only purchased it, but drew in my sketch pad the design you see in the picture.

quadruple loop chain

This is another chain that is easy to make and adaptable in both size and gauge. It also makes an excellent link for earrings, bracelets, and to add to other chain projects.

: materials

- 104-in. piece of 16-gauge round wire
- **44** 8mm outer diameter round open jump rings
- **2** 6mm large-hole round copper beads

: tools

- long-tined roundnose pliers
- 6mm bail-making pliers
- 9.5mm mandrel
- flatnose pliers
- chainnose pliers
- flush cutter
- small file or wire rounder
- chasing hammer
- bench block
- permanent marker
- ruler
- polishing cloth

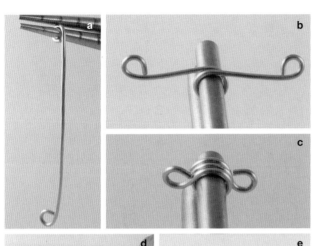

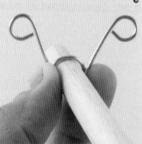

Links

1 Flush cut a 3½-in. piece of 16-gauge round wire.

2 Using roundnose pliers at the ½-in. plier mark, make a simple loop at each end of the wire. The loops should be on the same side of the wire **a**.

3 Using 6mm bail-making pliers, center the wire on the plier with the simple loops facing down toward the 8mm barrel. Bring each side of the wire around the 6mm barrel until the loops are directly across from each other **b**.

4 Wrap the wire around again until the loops are directly across from each other **c**.

5 Remove the link from the pliers and hammer the simple loops. Make 12 links.

6 Flush cut a 5¼-in. piece of 16-gauge round wire. Repeat steps 2–5, but use 6mm bail-making pliers in step 2 **d** and a 9.5mm mandrel in step 3 **e**, **f**. Make nine links.

7 At this point, you will have different size links **g**.

Clasp

8 Make a double-strength wrapped bead clasp, using a 6-in. piece of 16-gauge wire for the hook and a 6-in. piece of 16-gauge wire for the eye.

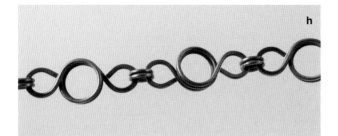

h

Finishing

9 Attach all the links using two jump rings. Place the nine larger links in the center of the chain and six of the smaller links on each side of the chain **h**.

10 Using two jump rings, attach the hook to one end and the eye to the other end of the chain.

11 Add patina, if desired, following manufacturer's instructions.

more ideas

▲ Colorful lampwork and onyx beads are mixed with the quadruple-loop links to create a necklace with multiple layers and dimension.

▶ Use one quadruple-looped link per earring and attach wrapped beads to make a stunning pair of earrings. For the wrapped beads, I used an adaptation of the Front-Drilled Onyx Circle Pendant p. 36.

◀ I used the quadruple-looped link centered and added two chains for a thicker cuff-like bracelet. I also made the spiraled hook and eye in a heavier gauge wire to match the thickness of the triple chain.

double strength wrapped bead clasp

Hook

1 Flush cut a 6-in. piece of 16-gauge round wire. Mark the center of the wire.

2 With 6mm bail-making pliers, make two wraps around the plier. Stop with the wire ends pointing away from each other **a**.

3 With flatnose pliers, bend one of the wires at a 90-degree angle to the other wire. With chainnose pliers, wrap the wire that faces out to the side, around the neck of the 90-degree wire one time **b**. Squeeze the wrap tight around the wire.

4 String a 6mm bead onto the wire **c**. Using chainnose pliers, wrap the wire around the bead once **d** and then around the top of the bead and back around the wire. Trim and tuck any excess.

5 With flatnose pliers, bend the remaining wire parallel to the double loop **e**.

6 Using 8mm bail-making pliers, make a loop for the hook **f**. Trim this wire even with the top of the last wrap. Gently hammer the hook and reshape it, if needed.

Eye

7 Flush cut a 6-in. piece of 16-gauge round wire. Mark the center of the wire.

8 Repeat steps 2–5 of Hook.

9 Using 6mm bail-making pliers, make a wrapped loop back up against the bead **g**. Trim this wire even with the top of the bead. Gently hammer the loop and reshape it, if needed.

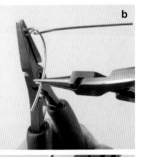

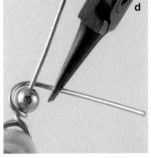

reversible top drilled marquee pendant

The beauty of this woven pendant is that it is reversible and requires very few materials to create.

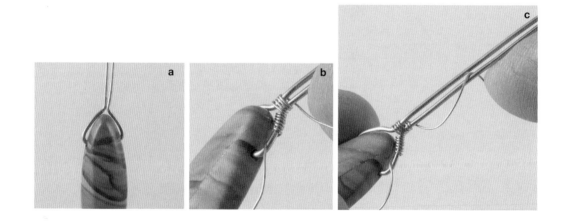

: materials

- 1¼-in. marquis top-drilled bead
- 15-in. piece of 20-gauge round wire
- 84-in. piece of 28-gauge round wire

: tools

- 6mm bail-making pliers or mandrel
- flatnose pliers
- chainnose pliers
- long-tined roundnose pliers
- flush cutter
- small file or wire rounder
- permanent marker
- ruler
- polishing cloth

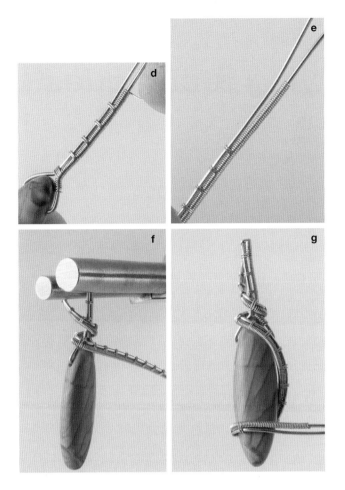

1 Flush cut a 15-in. piece of 20-gauge round wire and string the bead to the center of the wire.

2 Press and bend both sides of the wire over the bead. Using flatnose pliers, bend both wires parallel to each other at the top of the bead **a**.

3 Make six coils around base wire 1. Make four complete wraps around base wire 1 and 2 **b**.

4 Choose your weave pattern. I chose Weave 1 (p. 90). Make 10 coils around base wire 1 **c** and two complete wraps around base wire 1 and 2. Repeat this pattern **d**. Complete this weave rotation 24 times. Finish with 30 coils on base wire 1 **e**.

5 Mark ¾ in. from the top of the bead. With the 6mm bail-making pliers, grasp the wire at the mark.

6 Loop the wire around the plier and to the front. Wrap the wire around the top of the bead completely one time so that the wires are back to the front of the pendant **f**.

7 Bring the wires down along the side of the bead and to the back. Continue to bring the wire around the base of the bead **g**.

8 Wrap the wires around the base until you are at the tip of the bead.

9 Using chainnose pliers, make a spiral in the wires at the tip of the bead.

10 Add patina, if desired, following manufacturer's instructions.

more ideas

◄ For this ocean jasper bead, I added a small spiral in front and took my weave around one time for a more open style.

▶ This clear crystal bead intrigued me— was it a good wrapping candidate? Yes! I love the resulting see-through pendant.

◄ This tiny kyanite bead looks stunning in a simple silver weave and wrap.

▶ Use a small turquoise bead and 22-gauge base wire to create a dainty, feminine drop pendant.

advanced wireweaving techniques

These techniques and embellishments will help you create, personalize, and enhance your designs. Interchange and adapt them from project to project. Use them to add unique characteristics and dimensions to each pendant you design. You will find references to these techniques throughout the projects.

Coiling Chart
Gauge approximately how much wire you will need when coiling by referencing this chart.

BASE WIRE	COILING WIRE GAUGE	* INCHES (APPROXIMATE) OF WIRE NEEDED TO COVER AN INCH OF BASE WIRE
20 gauge	28 gauge	12 in.
	26 gauge	10½ in.
18 gauge	28 gauge	13 in.
	26 gauge	12 in.
16 gauge	26 gauge	15 in.
	24 gauge	13 in.

*Approximation includes a short tail at the beginning and end of the coiled wire When adding beads to the coil, decrease the wire amount by approximately ¹⁄₃₂ in. per 3mm bead.

coiling tips
- You need at least an 8-gauge size differential between the base wire and the coiling wire to ensure ease of coiling and a good coiled base wire-to-coiling wire ratio. For example, for a 20-gauge base wire, use a 28-gauge coiling wire.
- Use a small piece of rubber shelf liner to help hold the base wire if you have difficulty holding it still.
- Always try to cut the coiling wire so that it can be hidden and tucked in place.

Coiling

Learning to make wire coils is an essential wire jewelry technique. The trick to creating professional coils is to make sure all the coils are evenly wrapped, with no gaps or overlaps, and are tight against one another. Coiling can be done with a mandrel or directly onto your jewelry. All it takes is practice to master this important skill.

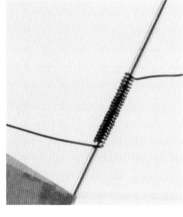

◀ Simple Coil

Load 28-gauge coiling wire onto a bobbin. Make a small bend at the end of the coiling wire. Hook the bend onto a 20-gauge base wire, and wrap the coiling wire three times around the base wire. Make the wrap nice and straight, and not at an angle. Continue wrapping the coiling wire five wraps at a time. Stop after each set of five wraps to ensure that they are straight and there are no gaps. If there are gaps, push the wraps together with your fingers. Once you've coiled all the wire to the desired length, trim and use chainnose pliers to press down the wire end. Check for burs or ends of wire poking out that could scratch or cause snags.

◀ Beaded Coil

Load 28-gauge coiling wire onto a bobbin. Make a small bend at the end of the wire. Hook the bend onto a 20-gauge base wire and wrap the coiling wire three times around the base wire. Make the wraps nice and straight and not at an angle. Continue wrapping the coiling wire five wraps at a time. Stop after each set of five wraps to ensure that they are straight and there are no gaps. If there are gaps, push the wraps down together with your fingers. String a bead onto the base wire **a**. Make a wrap over the bead and onto the base wire **b**. Continue making coiled wraps and adding beads. Once you've coiled all the wire to the desired length, trim and use chainnose pliers to press down the wire end. Check for burs or ends of wire poking out that could scratch or cause snags.

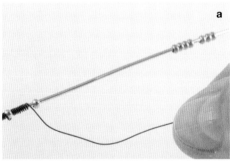

a

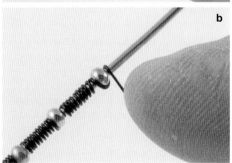

b

Wire Weaving Patterns

Wire weaving allows you to embellish and add dimension to your projects. By using fine wire gauges, such as 24–28, you will be able to weave to the best advantage for your design. Weaving is a technique that becomes easier the more you practice it. Weave patterns are repetitive and can be mixed and matched. Once you master the basics, your designs with weaving are unlimited. The weaves depicted are some of my favorites and are a good foundation as you learn.

Each weave has a picture and expanded weave examples as well an illustration. The base wires are numbered in the illustration and the numbering is referenced in the instructions. See also bobbin weaving p. 12.

Terms and Preparation

Base wire: the wire or wires onto which you weave, usually 6–8 gauges larger than the coiling or weave wire.
Weave wire: thinner gauge wire used to make weave patterns.

In all the weave pattern illustrations and photos, the base wires are 20-gauge round wire and the weave wires are 28-gauge round wire. I start each weave on base wire 1 with 3–5 coils to anchor the weave pattern.

To begin all weaves: Make a small bend at the end of the 28-gauge weave wire. Hook the bend onto the 20-gauge base wire 1 to begin the weave. Follow the weave instructions. Make the wraps nice and straight and not at an angle. If there are gaps, push the wraps together with your fingers. Once you've completed the weave to the desired length, trim and use chainnose pliers to press down the wire end. Check for burs or ends of wire poking out that could scratch or cause snags.

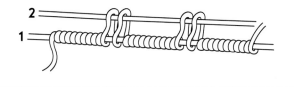

◀ Weave 1

Weave 1 is a versatile and easily adapted two base-wire weave. Change the look of this weave simply by adding or subtracting wraps on either base wire.

Wrap the weaving wire 10 times around base wire 1. Wrap the weaving wire twice completely around both base wires 1 and 2 Wrap 10 more times around base wire 1. This completes one rotation of the weave.

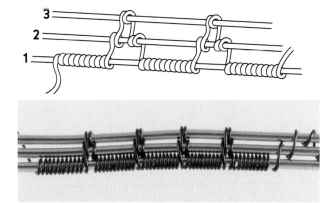

◀ Weave 2

Weave 2 is an excellent weave pattern for making bezels and encasing beads. You gain added strength and dimension using three base wires. As with Weave 1, you can easily change the look simply by adding or subtracting the wraps on either base wire.

Wrap the weave wire 10 times around base wire 1. Wrap the weaving wire once completely around base wire 2. Wrap once completely around base wire 3. On the backside of the base wires, wrap once completely around base wire 2 and then wrap once completely around base wire 1. Wrap 10 more times around base wire 1. This completes one rotation of the weave.

▶ Weave 3

Weave 3 is an excellent four-base wire stepped-wrap-capture weave that can be used to give strength and help maintain the shape of many woven jewelry designs.

Wrap the weave wire 10 times around base wire 1. Wrap completely around base wire 2 one time and go back down to base wire 1. Wrap 10 more times around base wire 1. In a step fashion, wrap one complete time around base wire 2, then base wire 3, then base wire 4. Bring the weave wire straight down the back and wrap 10 times around base wire 1. Push all the wraps together with your fingers. This completes one rotation of the weave.

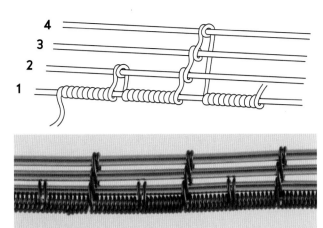

▶ Weave 4

Weave 4 is another very versatile and easily adapted two base-wire weave. Change the look of this weave simply by adding or subtracting the wraps on either base wire.

Hook the weave wire around base wire 1 and wrap five times. Wrap the weaving wire once completely around base wire 2 and carry the weave wire around to the back of base wire 2. Wrap one time completely around base wire 1. This completes one rotation of the weave.

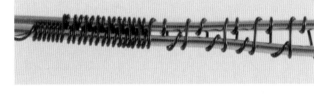

▶ Weave 5

Weave 5 is a three base-wire weave that can add depth and fullness. Change the look of this weave simply by adding or subtracting the wraps to either base wire.

Hook the weave wire around base wire 1 and wrap five times. Wrap the weaving wire once completely around both base wires 1 and 2. Repeat and wrap the weaving wire once completely around both base wires 1 and 2, then around base wire 2 and 3. Wrap the weaving wire once completely around both base wires 2 and 3. Wrap behind all the base wires and back to base wire 1. This completes one rotation of this weave. Be sure to press the weave pattern together as you go to help eliminate any gaps and keep your weave tight.

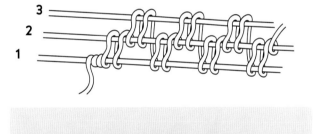

▶ Weave 6

Weave 6 is similar to the step wraps in weave 3.

Hook the weave wire onto base wire 1 and wrap five times. In a step fashion, wrap one complete time around base wire 2, and then base wire 3. Bring the weave wire straight down the back to base wire 1. This completes one rotation of the weave.

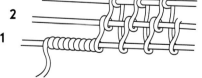

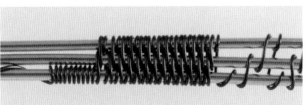

◀ Weave 7

Weave 7 is an excellent two base-wire weave that makes a good transition weave pattern.

Hook the weave wire onto base wire 1 and wrap 10 times. Wrap the weave wire completely around base wire 2 one time and go back to base wire 1. Wrap 10 times around base wire 1. This completes one weave rotation.

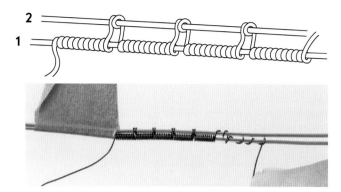

◀ Weave 8

Weave 8 makes a really nice two base-wire woven edge pattern.

Hook the bend onto base wire 1 and wrap the weave wire five times around base wire 1. Wrap the weave wire up and over base wire 1, between 1 and 2, then up and behind base wire 2. Wrap the weave wire around base wire 2, between 1 and 2. This creates a complete wrap around base wire 2. Make another wrap around base wire 2, and bring the weave wire between 2 and 1 and down behind base wire 1. This completes one rotation of the weave.

weaving tips

- Weave from the bottom base wire to the top base wire and left to right (just as you read).
- Keep good tension on your weave wire. As you can see in the basics section, the weave wire makes a tension groove on my guide finger as I weave. (See also bobbin weaving p. 12.)
- You need at least an 8-gauge size differential between the base wire and the weave wire to ensure ease of weaving and a good base wire to weave wire ratio. For a 20-gauge base wire, use 28-gauge weaving wire.
- If you do not have a bobbin to use for weaving or have to weave where it is not possible to use a bobbin, then work with about 3 ft. of weave wire at a time. Working with the shorter length will help you avoid tangles and kinks.
- If the base wires overlap as you weave, then you are using too much tension on the weave wire. Loosen up!
- To help avoid kinks, keep a smooth rounded loop as you pull the weave wire through or around the frame wire. Using a bobbin to weave helps enormously to avoid kinks.
- When weaving on a frame that has one end wider than the other, start your weave at the narrowest end. This will keep the wire from slipping down as you weave.
- Use a pick, wooden cuticle stick, or T pin to separate accidentally over-lapped weave wires, to make a small space to push a wire through, or to close gaps in your weave.
- When weaving, leave a wire-width of space between each base wire.

Creating Patterns

Generate an infinite number of your own unique weave patterns by mixing and matching weave patterns, adjusting the number and size of the wires, changing direction in the weave, or by adding separation weaves between each pattern. To create a repeating pattern, simply create a sequence of weaves and then repeat that sequence over and over. To create a random weave, simply weave patterns in no particular order and have no repeating sequences. Experiment with weave patterns to find the ones that best suit your style and needs.

design & inspiration

Your project design is usually the starting place and will guide your choices of stones, beads, glass, crystals, or metals. Or, the materials will guide the textures and character of your piece. Many times I have sat just looking at my beads, stones, and wire simply thinking about where to start. Many students ask me, "How do I know where to start or what to make?" So, here, I present my thinking process and the steps I ponder when designing my jewelry.

I use a variety of wireworking techniques. Through wrapping, weaving, and manipulating the wire, I can incorporate unique patterns and shapes as well as stones, beads, and other elements. I constantly look for new ways of using and combining these techniques so that I may follow through with my design ideas. It is my goal to design a creative piece of jewelry that is functional, beautiful, and unique. My inspiration comes from many sources: beautiful stones, shapes in nature, ancient jewelry and artifacts, Alexander Calder's whimsical work with jewelry, and other mediums such as painting or sculpture.

Like many designers, I follow a simple method for organizing my thoughts from concept to completion.

1 First, I start by sketching my idea…
and my sketches are not perfect or beautiful. I try to draw as many variations or types of jewelry as I could possibly make with my idea, such as earrings, pendants, and bracelets. I prefer to sketch on file folders because they are stiffer and easier to store. I can place parts and materials inside the folder to keep as I work. I even use them to cut out templates of jewelry designs I would like to try out. When I am away from home, I carry and use a sketch journal to capture any inspirations and ideas. Upon returning home, I transfer them to a file folder. Often times I sketch my idea true-to-size using graph paper, so I can get a fairly good estimate of how many links I may need for a particular chain or approximately how much wire I might require for a pendant.

2 Next, I pick or design components
that I will incorporate into my jewelry, such as beads, stones, cabs, metals, and so on. Many times I trace the shapes of the stones or elements onto my sketch and use colored pencils to add color. This gives me a good idea of how the finished piece might look and also can make it obvious that I need to make a color, shape, or size adjustment. Since I love design components that add a touch of surprise, such as an asymmetrical shape or an unusual color palette, I also incorporate such things into my sketch.

3 Then, I visualize and sketch the steps and
techniques needed to complete the piece. I take into account the stones and components I will use, as well as the gauges and kinds of metals that will make my piece aesthetically pleasing.

4 Many times, I make a prototype of
the piece of jewelry based on my design sketch and chosen components.

5 At this point I begin fabrication. Many
of my designs morph as I fabricate them because I continually adjust and rethink my design elements as I progress. Sometimes my design sketch can take me in a new direction. This is why every piece is unique and why my final piece of jewelry may not always match my original sketch.

6 Often times I complete steps 1—3,
only to put my sketch away for another day. One time, I sketched a small cross pendant colored with a multitude of beads and stones. I put away the sketch and several months later pulled it back out but instead, developed a very large holiday wall cross. My design idea had totally morphed.

acknowledgments

Thanks to my husband, Blake Berlin for his constant support and encouragement of my work; Curtis Potter for his photography skills and help; and my family for their encouragement throughout this project. I would also like to thank my editor, Karin Van Voorhees and the fabulous Kalmbach team for their invaluable help and support.

about the author

Designing wireworked jewelry gives Kimberly Sciaraffa Berlin a creative outlet and great satisfaction. She finds it both relaxing and rewarding to work on and complete her projects. Kimberly chooses to incorporate a wide variety of metals, glass, crystals, beads, wire, semi-precious stones, and cabochons to create her unique pieces. She is predominately self-taught and her designs are greatly influenced by ancient art, nature, Alexander Calder, and other artistic mediums. She feels that Calder's jewelry creations have inspired her to think and design without limit.

Kimberly has been published in *Bead & Button* magazine, *Wirework* magazine, *Creative Chain Mail Jewelry*, and *Creative Beading*. Her first book, *Build Your Own Wire Pendants*, was published in 2012. When she isn't teaching jewelry making or showing her jewelry at a jewelry show, she enjoys rock hunting, reading, and crafting.

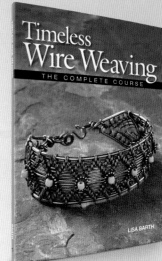

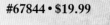